ROOT CROP PROCESSING

ENERGY AND ENVIRONMENT TECHNOLOGY SOURCE BOOKS

Electricity in Households and Micro-enterprises
Energy Efficiency
Rural Transport
Water Supply

FOOD CYCLE TECHNOLOGY SOURCE BOOKS

Cereal Processing
Dairy Processing
Drying
Fish Processing
Fruit and Vegetable Processing
Oil Processing
Packaging
Root Crop Processing
Storage
Women's Roles in Technical Innovation

Food Cycle Technology Source Books

ROOT CROP PROCESSING

in association with the
United Nations Development Fund for Women (UNIFEM) 1993

Acknowledgement

This series of Food cycle technology source books has been prepared at the Intermediate Technology Development Group (ITDG) in the United Kingdom within the context of UNIFEM's Women and Food Cycle Technologies specialization.

During the preparation process the project staff contacted numerous project directors, rural development agencies, technology centres, women's organizations, equipment manufacturers and researchers in all parts of the world.

The authors wish to thank the many agencies and individuals who have contributed to the preparation of this source book. Special thanks are owed to the International Labour Organization (ILO), the Food and Agriculture Organization of the United Nations (FAO), the United Nations Children's Fund (UNICEF), the Economics Commission for Africa (ECA), the German Appropriate Technology Exchange (GATE/GTZ), the Groupe de Recherche et d'Echanges Technologiques (GRET), the Royal Tropical Institute (KIT), the International Development Research Centre (IDRC), the Natural Resources Institute (NRI), Appropriate Technology International (ATI), The Institute of Development Studies at Sussex University (IDS), and the Save the Children Fund.

The preparation of the source books was funded by UNIFEM with a cost-sharing contribution from the Government of Italy and the Government of the Netherlands. UNIFEM is also grateful to the Government of Italy, via the Italian Association of Women in Development (AIDOS), for sponsoring the translation of this series into French and Portuguese, and the printing of the first editions.

Barrie Axtell   *Linda Adams*
IT Consultants   UNIFEM

Practical Action Publishing Ltd
27a Albert Street, Rugby, CV21 2SG, Warwickshire, UK
www.practicalactionpublishing.org

First published by Practical Action Publishing in 1995
Reprinted in 2002
Transferred to digital printing in 2008

ISBN 978 1 85339 138 5

UNIFEM was created during the United Nations Decade for Women to provide technical and financial support to benefit rural and poor urban women in developing countries.
Address: 304 East 45th Street, New York, NY 10017, USA.

Since 1974, Practical Action Publishing has published and disseminated books and information in support of international development work throughout the world. Practical Action Publishing is a trading name of Practical Action Publishing Ltd (Company Reg. No. 1159018), the wholly owned publishing company of Practical Action. Practical Action Publishing trades only in support of its parent charity objectives and any profits are covenanted back to Practical Action (Charity Reg. No. 247257, Group VAT Registration No. 880 9924 76).

Illustrations by Peter Dobson, UK
Typeset by Inforum, Rowlands Castle, Hants, UK

Contents

PREFACE   vi

INTRODUCTION   vii

1 Pre-processing and processing considerations   1

Raw materials   1
Principles of processing techniques   2
Socio-economic considerations   4

2 Traditional processing techniques and equipment   7

Traditional equipment   7
Potato   8
Yam   10
Edible aroids   12
Sweet potato   13
Cassava   15
Traditional curing methods   19

3 Improved processing equipment and products   20

Peeling and washing   21
Grating and rasping   24
Pounding   27
Pressing and de-watering   28
Sieving   31
Roasting   32
Drying   34
Milling and grinding   36
Chipping and slicing   37

4 Case studies   41

5 Planning a project or enterprise   46

REFERENCES   49

FURTHER READING   49

CONTACTS   52

Preface

This source book is one of a continuing UNIFEM series which aims to increase awareness of the range of technological options and sources of expertise, as well as indicating the complex nature of designing and successfully implementing technology development and dissemination programmes.

UNIFEM was established in 1976, and is an autonomous body associated since 1984 with the United Nations Development Programme. UNIFEM seeks to free women from under-productive tasks and augment the productivity of their work as a means of accelerating the development process. It does this through funding specific women's projects which yield direct benefits and through actions directed to ensure that all development policies, plans, programmes and projects take account of the needs of women producers.

In recognition of women's special roles in the production, processing, storage, preparation and marketing of food, UNIFEM initiated a Food Cycle Technology project in 1985 with the aim of promoting the widespread diffusion of tested technologies to increase the productivity of women's labour in this sector. While global in perspective, the initial phase of the project was implemented in Africa in view of the concern over food security in many countries of the region.

A careful evaluation of the Africa experience in the final phase of this five-year programme showed that there was a need for catalytic interventions which would lead to an enabling environment for women to have easier access to technologies. This would be an environment where women producers can obtain information on the available technologies, have the capacity to analyse such information, make technological choices on their own, and acquire credit and training to enable the purchase and operation of the technology of their choice. This UNIFEM source book series aims to facilitate the building of such an environment.

Introduction

THIS BOOK covers the small-scale processing of tropical root crops in developing countries, with the intention of providing consultants with some technical understanding of traditional and improved technologies for use in these countries.

An illustration of the wider context into which projects may be introduced (in terms of socio-economic issues) is also given. This should enable consultants to see any merits and/or problems likely to follow the introduction of technologies to different groups in various developing countries. In such countries, the family meals are usually prepared by women who are therefore involved in the various stages of processing the raw material for consumption.

Root crops are a staple and hence are often the main part of the meal, especially where cereals are unavailable. Village-scale processing of root crops is therefore an important part of women's daily work. A substantial effort has been made to upgrade local processes, but many communities still only have access to traditional methods which although appropriate are laborious.

Large-scale production of starches, glucose syrups, animal feeds, gari etc. from root crops is a commercial venture involving substantial capital investment. For direct human consumption, the processing of root crops is mainly on a small scale, often household level.

It would be impossible to cover all the root crops and processing techniques in a book of this size, so the more common methods of processing the more important root crops — cassava, yam, sweet potato, potato and edible aroids — are discussed.

Emphasis is placed on cassava throughout this manual for several reasons. Even though the total world production for sweet potato may perhaps be greater, cassava's prime importance as a food in Africa, and the fact that it often requires special treatment to make it fit for human consumption, means that there is a greater variety of processing methods. Finally, small-scale cassava processing in developing countries has been researched and developed to a greater degree than any other root crop.

This book is divided into several sections covering basic food science principles; traditional and improved small-scale processing methods and equipment relevant to rural women; case studies illustrating the merits and problems of introducing improved technologies into a particular socio-economic framework; a list of summarizing questions placing processing in the wider context of village situations, and a list of institutions to contact for information. It is important to realize that although a technology may be improved and tested technically in a research laboratory, workshop or field situation outside any community, it may prove inappropriate for the intended social setting. Although it is realized that one can only discover the outcome of introducing a technology by trying it, it should be borne in mind that assumptions can be made more accurately if consideration is first given to the reality — that is, rural women need recognition and access to relevant institutions, infrastructural support, extension workers and formal lines of credit.

Importance of root crops

The most important root crops in terms of tonnage production in developing countries are cassava, potato and sweet potato. There seems to be some disagreement over which is the most important, some sources favouring sweet potato (Table 1), others cassava, but this is a point of academic interest. While other major crops such as yams and co-coyams are important foods in certain areas, their levels of production are considerably less.

It is estimated that 65 per cent of cassava produced is for direct food use, the remainder being used in animal feed (30 per cent) or processed into industrial products (5 per cent). Reliable data on the ratios of other major root crops used for food and industrial uses are not readily available. Root crops are a cheap, readily available and essential energy source for many poor people who face problems of food availability. Although they contain little protein or fat, some, particularly sweet potato and yam, are a source of vital vitamins (A and C).

Over half of the world's total cassava production is in Africa (Table 2), and it has been estimated that 37 per cent of the energy in the diet in tropical Africa comes from cassava. In the Americas and Asia the contribution is estimated to be only 12 per cent and 7 per cent respectively. Tropical root crops are mainly consumed and, where necessary processed at the village and household level. The relative importance of individual root crops varies both by region and country. Yams are a major food crop in West Africa, the Caribbean, the South Pacific Islands, South-east Asia, India and parts of Brazil. Cassava is particularly important in South America, West, East, Central and South Africa, and Oceania. Taro plays an important cultural role in the diet of the people of the Pacific Islands, as does sweet potato in part of West Africa, Oceania and the West Indies. Potato, requiring a more temperate climate, is more important in highland areas of the tropics such as the Andean regions of Peru and Bolivia. The main advantages of root crops as a staple compared with cereals are that they are a cheaper source of energy, can be cultivated easily and provide more dietary energy per hectare at a lower cost to the farmer (principally because of reduced labour inputs). They generally require a comparatively low level of husbandry, especially cassava which can grow in very dry and nutrient-deficient soils, albeit with lower yields.

Some root crops have a production cycle which is continuous or semi-continuous, in contrast to cereal production, where harvesting is highly seasonal. Taro and cassava, for example, are grown in the tropics all year round. This can avoid storage problems and can provide increased food security for the poor, especially during periods of food shortage. The continuous cropping of root crops to act as a reserve food buffer allows many poor people to survive better the problems of seasonality and shortages of other food items. It should be noted, however, that the practice of only partially harvesting certain root crops and relying on their natural underground storage can create a problem of land availability for subsistence farmers.

The pre-harvest period of, for example, cereals is often the most difficult time for poor people. Not only can it be a 'hungry' period, but food prices are generally higher, food intake is at its lowest and labour requirements on the farm are rising in anticipation of harvest. The role of root crops at such times is thus of prime importance.

Women's role in processing

The majority of the labour required for the processing of all root crops is provided

Table 1. Value of production of ten principal food crops in all developing countries

	Number of producing countries	Production (million tonnes)	Producer price ($ per tonne)	Value (billion $)
Rice	97	383	170	65
Wheat	69	162	148	24
Maize	119	154	119	18
Potatoes	98	91	142	13
Sweet potatoes	100	137	89	12
Cassava	95	127	70	9
Banana/plantain	119	62	107	7
Sorghum	69	44	123	5
Peanuts (Groundnuts)	92	17	297	5
Millet	53	27	144	4

(Horton, Fano, 1985)

Table 2. Cassava: area and production in selected countries

	Area harvested ('000)			Production ('000 t)		
	1974–6 average	1983	1984	1974–6 average	1983	1984
World	12207	13489	14151	107679	123048	129020
Africa	6438	7191	7482	43300	48593	51002
Angola	121	130	130	1710	1950	1950
Ghana	253	210	250	1773	1729	1900
Mozambique	533	500	550	2600	3150	3150
Nigeria	1043	1150	1250	10467	9950	11800
Tanzania	707	450	450	5053	5400	5600
Zaire	1687	2086	2150	11734	14600	14800
South America	2549	2500	2311	30587	26979	26861
Brazil	2047	2023	1817	25453	21569	21275
Colombia	246	207	210	1998	2000	2100
Asia	3048	3615	4171	32713	46450	50000
China	197	252	252	2416	3880	4067
India	383	302	305	6462	5341	5800
Indonesia	1424	1242	1420	12589	12229	14000
Thailand	538	1018	1335	7855	18989	19985
All developing countries	12207	13489	14151	107679	123048	129020

(FAO, 1984)

by women. It must be remembered, however, that the simple provision of labour does not ensure that women derive the benefits from a particular process. That depends much more on who controls the process — who makes the decisions on time allocation and the distribution of benefits gained. This control can sometimes lie with the grower of the crop rather than the processors or those who market the final product.

In some countries production and processing of a root crop is under women's control (e.g. cassava in West Africa), while in other regions it is a male prestige crop and taboo for women to cultivate it (as, for example, with certain yams in Nigeria and a specific variety of swamp taro in the Pacific Islands).

It is important to take these considerations of control into account in any project. Let us imagine, for example, a situation where the man grows a crop on land he controls, while women process the produce of that land. If the man invests in a labour-saving process so that he can re-deploy his wife in the fields, saving him time, who has really benefited? The community as a whole, yes, if the men can use their freed-up time productively; but the women have not benefited, at least not directly.

In the case where the land, labour and material inputs are sufficiently under the woman's control, labour-saving technological improvements may have more direct impact on her own and her family's livelihoods. It has been seen that even when women farmers control these inputs, they can suffer displacement with the introduction of mechanization. For example, in parts of West Africa the introduction of motorized cassava graters has greatly improved the productivity of gari processing, making this an attractive economic activity to both men and women. It has been known that the farming of cassava, once a 'women's crop', has been taken over by male members within a household, with the females having to look for alternative income opportunities once the production became mechanized.

It is vital that the women processors themselves are included in project design and implementation. Women producers are always trying to maximize their limited resources. It is vital to understand how they value these resources and the trade-offs they are willing to make in their distribution. Experience has shown that some technologies have not been accepted because they have not taken into account the perceived needs and priorities of the user.

Project design, therefore, should look beyond the immediate confines of the 'project'. The processing activity should be seen as part of a number of systems: firstly, a food production system of growing, processing and marketing; secondly, an economic system of production and exchange, and thirdly, a social system of interactions between members of the same family, between families, sexes and clans, in the same community and between communities. Only then can a reasonable assessment of the likely distribution of benefits of introducing an improved technology be made.

1
Pre-processing and processing considerations

IT IS IMPORTANT to have a basic understanding of the physiology of any crop in order to be able to predict its post-harvest behaviour. This, together with a knowledge of certain essential food science principles and the chemical composition of the crop, will put the consultant in a far better position to study and adapt a given processing system.

In this book, it will only be necessary to describe the general composition of root crops together with basic food science principles relevant to their processing. Socio-economic aspects of farming tropical root crops will also be discussed.

Raw materials

Root crops, as the name implies, are plants that develop starchy roots, tubers, stems, bulbs or corms which act as a food store for the plant. Chemically, they are mainly composed of water and starch with minor amounts of protein, fibre, minerals, vitamins and, very importantly in some cases, toxic components.

The term 'root crops' can be somewhat misleading and, in this publication, will cover commodities such as cassava, yams, potatoes, sweet potatoes and certain aroids all of which are staple food crops of high starch content. Aroids, such as taro and tannia (known collectively as coco-yams in Africa), in which the starch is deposited in swollen stems are included for convenience with root crops. Bananas, plantains and other staple starchy fruits, while processed in ways very similar to root crops, are not covered in this publication but rather in the relevant fruit and vegetable volume. After the plant has finished growing and the foliage dies away, the 'food store' of many root crops survives by going into dormancy, the duration of which depends on both the crop type and variety. Cassava is the exception, having no natural dormancy period.

The post-harvest storage life of a root crop thus depends on the type of crop as well, of course, as the conditions of storage. The end of post-harvest storage is signalled by sprouting and the removal of the sprouts can, in many cases, increase the storage period. This is particularly true of yams.

In addition to the main chemical components, such as starch, root crops contain important minor components. One of these is an enzyme called polyphenyloxidase, which causes the well-known darkening effect of fresh cut surfaces on exposure to air. This effect, which can be controlled by the use of chemicals, or blanching in hot water or steam, needs to be taken into consideration in certain processing systems.

As several root crops contain toxic substances, the most important being a cyanide-containing glycoside in cassava, and solanins in some varieties of potato, special processing procedures are required to make the product safe for human consumption. The cyanogenic glycoside complex in cassava can produce extremely toxic hydrogen cyanide through the action of natural enzymes in the root. Levels of hydrogen cyanide range from 10 to over 450mg/kg of fresh root depending upon variety. In many countries consumers often distinguish between sweet (of low toxicity) and bitter (of high toxicity) cassava. It is important to realize that although many sweet varieties do have lower levels of cyanide there is no well-defined correlation between the sweet/bitter taste and toxicity (Cooke, 1978). Considerable care should thus be taken when introducing unfamiliar varieties of sweet cassava to be sure that it is indeed a low cyanide variety.

Should cassava containing cyanide be consumed, the body will attempt to detoxify it. This puts the body system under great strain and can pose a serious health problem. The problem is particularly serious in areas with a low intake of dietary iodine (in which case goitre can develop) and for consumers with a low protein intake. The toxic glycosides of cassava are reduced to safer levels during traditional processing.

Toxicity is initially considerably reduced by peeling. The roots are then grated, breaking down the internal cells and so releasing the enzyme which starts to break down the cyanogenic glycoside complex. This releases hydrogen cyanide. During the subsequent fermentation stage, almost total breakdown of the glycoside occurs and the final frying, roasting or boiling step drives off the hydrogen cyanide, leaving a safer, edible product.

Toxicity problems have also been mentioned with regard to certain varieties of potato. This is of less importance on a worldwide basis and traditional methods have been developed to make the product safer for human consumption. Toxic varieties of potatoes are most commonly grown at high altitudes, particularly in the Andes. After harvesting they are soaked in water which removes the toxic components. The leached potatoes are then suitable for further processing, most commonly into a dried potato product. This process is described in more detail in Chapter 2.

Principles of processing techniques

A number of operations are commonly used in the processing of root crops and a brief summary of them is included below. The descriptions are not intended to be crop-specific and fuller details will be found in the relevant sections on traditional and improved root crop processing.

Peeling

This involves the removal of the indigestible outer layers of the root and is traditionally carried out by hand, although mechanical and chemical peelers are available for larger-scale operations.

Drying

It has been noted that root crops have a high moisture content. The preservation of almost all processed root crop products depends on reducing the moisture to a level which prevents the growth of microorganisms. Drying is a very simple, inexpensive and common method of removing water in root crops and so extending their shelf-life. A brief summary of the principles involved is included here. Specific drying technologies are covered later in this book.

Drying requires the transfer of moisture from the product to the air around it. Clearly both the quantity (air flow) and moisture content (relative humidity) of the air will affect the rate at which a product dries, as will the nature of the product itself.

It is important to realize that there are two stages in the drying process:
(1) removing 'surface moisture'.
(2) removing 'internal moisture' from within the material.

The relative humidity of air decreases rapidly as its temperature is raised and at the same time its water-absorbing capacity increases.

The rate of drying during the first stage is dependent solely on the ability of the air passing over the material to absorb and remove moisture.

Air-flow rate is more important than temperature but in areas of high relative humidity the air may need heating to lower its humidity to a level that allows it to absorb significant amounts of water. In general, air with a relative humidity of 75 per cent or more is not able to effect drying except in the earliest stages when the root is very wet.

The surface area of food exposed to the air is also very important. Slicing or chipping the root crop will increase the surface area, and thereby reduce the drying time.

Once the surface water is removed, a second stage of drying begins in which water is removed from the interior of the material. The rate of drying in this second stage is dependent on the rate at which moisture can migrate through the tissue to the surface where it evaporates to the passing air. The migration is a slow process, so drying rates are lower than in the first stage of drying. The drying rate is dependent on the moisture content, and on temperature, rather than air flow.

Boiling and steaming

Root crops are often cooked by boiling or steaming, either for direct consumption or as one step in a processing system. This does not preserve the crop, which is usually eaten soon afterwards, unless it is further processed. Boiling and steaming are also important in cassava processing, partially to detoxify the material.

Frying and roasting

Many types of root crops are commonly prepared by frying in hot oil or roasting. Roasting is widely practised throughout Africa where traditional techniques include burying the whole root in hot ashes or holding it in front of a fire. In gari processing, proper roasting is important to ensure a good quality product. Both frying and roasting enhance the flavour of the root crop and most importantly reduce its moisture content, so extending its shelf-life.

When packaged properly, fried, crisp products can have a shelf-life of several months.

Grating

The action of grating into fine shreds is a step common to the processing of many root crops and facilitates later steps in a process, for example, de-watering, drying or pulping. The process alters the texture of the raw material. Grating methods range from simply rasping the roots on the trunk-spines of palms as practised in the Amazon basin of South America, through simple hand-graters to mechanized graters.

Pounding

Pounding changes the texture of the previously prepared root crop to a more palatable, paste-like consistency. The root is first peeled and softened by boiling or soaking. Traditionally, a large pestle and mortar is used.

De-watering

De-watering, as the name implies, involves the removal of internal liquid from the root crop by pressing. This process is most common in cassava processing being an important method of reducing toxicity.

Traditionally, heavy weights are placed on the prepared root crop and the expelled liquid is allowed to drain away. A squeezing process is also involved in other traditional methods.

Starch extraction

While starch can be extracted from any root crop, the most common starting materials are potato and cassava. Industrially, starch is extracted by a combination of wet milling, sieving and either settling or centrifuging. Starch can also be extracted by simpler methods. The juice draining from cassava, for example, during de-watering may be collected and left to stand allowing the starch to settle. After decanting the liquid layer the remaining starch may be rinsed and further processed into flour by pounding or grinding and drying.

Grinding, milling and sieving

After preliminary processing, including slicing or shredding and drying, most root crops can be ground to a flour. Of all root crops cassava is most commonly processed in this way, the flour being used in many traditional dishes such as 'fufu'. Traditionally, pestles and mortars are used for pulverization but on a larger scale, hand or mechanical plate or disc mills are more appropriate. After grinding, the coarse flour is sieved, with any large particles returned for further grinding.

Fermentation

Fermentation is a most important step in the processing of cassava and certain high alkaloid-containing varieties of potato. In both cases fermentation results in a reduction in the levels of the toxic components. In the case of cassava, two methods are commonly practised, which may be conveniently considered as the 'dry' and 'wet' methods.

The dry method is used in the production of 'gari' and is essentially fermentation in the presence of air. The grated cassava passes through a two-stage fermentation. During the first phase, starch is broken down and acids are produced. Subsequently, breakdown in the cyanide containing toxic component occurs by the action of naturally occurring enzymes in the root so releasing hydrogen cyanide. The conditions at the end of this first stage then allow the growth of a range of micro-organisms that produce compounds that give gari its characteristic flavour. Much of the cyanide is lost during fermentation, the remainder being largely driven off during the final roasting step.

The simple 'wet' method of fermentation is carried out in certain areas of Africa and Latin America and is sometimes referred to as 'retting'. Wet fermentation takes place in the absence of air. Cassava roots, either peeled or entire, are soaked under water for several days until they have softened. The material is then broken up, sieved and finally squeezed to remove water. Although culturally acceptable in many areas, cassava processed in this way has a somewhat unpleasant odour and the waters used in the process can be a source of pollution in streams.

Socio-economic considerations

In general, traditionally processed root crops are low-value products which do not normally justify improved technologies with higher capital costs unless losses can be greatly reduced or higher-value products made. When considering establishing or improving a root processing system a decision on the production scale and technology used must be made. This decision will depend on:

o economic status of members of the community;
o supply of raw materials;
o labour requirements;
o cultural obstacles;
o organizational and management capabilities;
o availability of markets, both local and distant.

Economic status

It is a truism that no one can control a technology they do not own. This is, however, often forgotten in project work, when technologies are introduced that could not possibly be afforded by the groups being worked with.

This economic status is not simply the money people have to spend but also their access to credit. Most people can obtain access to credit, of a sort, but usually at extortionate interest rates. Any economic calculations must take this into account. Commercial interest rates (e.g. the bank rate in the capital) should not be used in calculations of rates of return unless the processors can really have access to money at those rates.

At the village level, payback periods of more than one agricultural cycle or year may be unrealistic because it means scarce cash resources will be unavailable for other, possibly more immediate needs.

Lengthy payback periods may prove to be an effective obstacle for poorer, more vulnerable households.

Raw materials

The supply of raw materials is particularly important. Technological improvements which require a high capital investment, such as a motorized cassava grater, will necessitate relatively high and stable crop production levels in order to pay for themselves within a reasonable time period.

Local land ownership patterns may preclude the establishment of a sufficient area under root crop cultivation. For example, in parts of West Africa, the community is traditionally the owner of the land with the chief allocating parcels of land to households as needed. In Sierra Leone, lack of regular access to fertile land to produce the necessary cassava supplies for a women's cassava grater group proved to be a major hindrance to expansion. In this case, competing requests for the land needed to cultivate cash crops by their male counterparts resulted in the women's group receiving lower priority.

Labour considerations

Labour requirements must be considered when choosing a technology, as they can vary for different crops at pre-harvest and post-harvest production time. When comparing expected labour demands for root crops like cassava and yams, cassava requires little labour and is very easy to cultivate whereas yams require considerable effort in such tasks as, for example, staking and drainage preparation. In terms of post-harvest production needs, cassava processing is perhaps the most demanding of all the root crops as it requires detoxification before becoming edible. Much less effort is required in processing yams, for example, which also have the advantage of being a relatively hardy crop that can be stored for several months before any processing is required.

Cultural obstacles

Group ownership and operation, which is needed to share investment costs and make maximum use of a higher capital cost technology, may meet local cultural obstacles. Women may need to ask their husband's permission to participate in work efforts outside the household. If the husband feels threatened by his wife's participation in an income-generating project or feels that her labour may be better used to support his cash activities, then this permission may not be granted.

In some areas or countries, women have a tradition of working co-operatively, but not of dividing tasks between themselves. The introduction of a technology that requires group co-operation may result in increased suspicion over pooled finances and fear of unequal compensation for labour input.

Organizational and management capabilities

If a new technology requires group organization, then there are several key questions that the members of the group must address themselves to:

o how will decisions be made?
o who will have access to the technology and on what terms?
o how will the group be managed from day to day?
o who will look after the money?
o who will operate and maintain the equipment?
o how will mis-use of funds or machinery be controlled?

As well as deciding on the constitution, the group will have to choose a manager, and she will have to be trained in her responsibilities and relevant skills. She must also be ready for much suspicion and must, therefore, be scrupulously honest. It is usual, and often unwise, that a village leader is chosen. She, or sometimes he, is often tempted to abuse his/her position, since no one will speak out in protest until it is too late.

Marketing potential

Processed root crop products such as cassava flour, flaked instant yam, breakfast and weaning foods, chip and snack products have been developed in response to an expanding demand from urban-based populations in developing countries. This has offered new opportunities for rural people to earn cash incomes from processing their root crops. These new products, however, while having great potential for adding value to root crops and providing income to rural producers, often have very limited markets. Any introduction of a new product must be accompanied by market research and consumer testing.

Along with these changes in consumer preference by an emerging middle class, there are growing health dangers as a result of rising demand. For example, in Nigeria, increased demand for the fermented cassava product, gari, has resulted in less careful processing. The fermentation period in certain zones is usually two to three days which allows sufficient time for breakdown of toxic elements within the cassava. Some commercial processors have reduced this period to one day and have added lime juice to produce the preferred sour taste instead of allowing the production of the natural fermented taste to occur in the detoxification process.

2
Traditional processing techniques and equipment

TRADITIONAL PROCESSING OF root crops has developed to suit local situations. A whole range of processing techniques, equipment and products have been developed which vary not only from country to country but also within individual countries. It would not be feasible to describe all the variations that exist, so in this section we shall look at typical processing systems used in Africa, Asia and Latin America. A description of some traditional equipment is followed by an account of traditional processing methods, covering the more common products in the three regions. The products described are arranged by crop type. In view of the emphasis on cassava so far, the following sections will start by looking at some of the other important root crops.

Before recommending methods for improving traditional processing systems, it is essential to understand fully how and why they have developed, how they fit into local social conditions and the relevant food science principles outlined earlier. Simply being aware of traditional practices is not enough.

Traditional equipment

The items described below are very simple, low in cost and available locally. These important factors determine the suitability of equipment to local processors. Most of the items have been designed for cassava processing because of the more elaborate procedures involved in making this crop safer to eat.

Peelers

Peeling of roots is commonly carried out using knives made of bamboo, flint or metal.

Graters

Examples of the wide range of traditional graters used particularly for cassava include, in South America, rough stone, the prickly trunk of palms, and shells. A stone or piece of wood covered with shark skin, or sharp stones set in basket-work, have been used in the West Indies. Graters made from flat pieces of wood into which splinters of thorn, teeth or fishbone are driven or embedded in a wax coating are used in Venezuela, parts of the Amazon and Brazil.

In Ghana, Nigeria and Sierra Leone graters are made from sheets of tin or iron which have been pierced with nails on one side in order to produce a rough surface on the other.

Presses

The 'Tipiti' is used in Latin America, particularly in Brazil, for de-watering cassava. It is a complex cylindrical basket press which is diagonally woven such that it can be stretched lengthwise to squeeze its contents. It is suspended from a beam or tree while the lower loop is weighted down with a stone, or a pole is inserted so that pressure can be exerted by pulling. More simply, strips of bark are spirally wrapped around the grated cassava and twisted to squeeze the contents.

Such devices are not found in Africa, where bags filled with cassava pulp are commonly pressed with heavy stones.

Sieves

Woven baskets or suspended cloth pieces holding the mash are used to allow the liquid to drain away or separate excess fibrous material.

Pounding/grinding equipment

In South America and Africa pestles and mortars made of heavy wood are used to pound both fresh roots prior to processing and also to produce flours. Some of these mortars may be large enough to require as many as eight women pounding simultaneously.

Roasters

A whole range of systems are used to roast root crop products over a fire. Examples include pans, oil drums cut in half and specially constructed raised clay semi-circles common in Nigeria. As the material is roasted, it is continuously turned with a wooden spoon.

Potato

Potatoes, unlike the other root crops covered in this source book, grow best at temperatures below 20°C. Production in developing countries is therefore concentrated in highland areas where the soil temperature is cool enough. Potatoes and their processed products are one of the staple foods of highland peoples such as those of the Andean areas of Peru and Bolivia.

Generally, potato is consumed fresh, that is to say by cooking the fresh tuber. However, this crop is seasonal and for supplies to be available out of season, it is necessary either to store fresh or to process it into a stable product. Dehydrated products such as 'papa seca' and 'chuño', which can have a storage life of several years, have been made for centuries in the Andean areas of Peru and Bolivia.

Potato is more difficult to cultivate than cassava because a live tuber, or seed, is required for planting the following season's crop. This seed potato thus has to be carefully stored and is more perishable than the stick, or stem used for cassava cultivation.

Potatoes can contain toxic complex alkaloids, termed solanines. The amount of solanine present depends on variety. Levels are higher in immature potatoes and particularly high in active growing parts of the plant such as sprouts. Bitter potatoes, with high levels of solanines, are grown in the high areas of the Andes and these are made safer for eating by processing into products such as chuño, tokosh and tunta.

To summarize, the main constraints facing potato production and marketing in developing countries are: its irregular yields, seasonality, availability of live tubers for planting and the perishability of the fresh tuber in normal tropical temperatures.

Traditionally processed products

Product	Chuño
Region	South America
Country	Peru
Equipment	Straw, rocks, sacks or pails.

Process	Process requires particular climatic conditions with very low night temperatures (–10 to –20°C), high day temperatures (20 to 25°C) and low relative humidity. Many variations in technique exist, the following is a typical method.
Raw material	Usually bitter varieties of potato.
Preparation	Laid on straw bed for one day.
Frozen	Potatoes laid out to freeze at night time.
Defrosted	The following day they are allowed to thaw and may be covered with straw to prevent blackening. This freezing and thawing process is repeated several times and causes rupturing of cells.
Treading	The potatoes are trampled, so squeezing out liquid from the broken cells and removing the skin.
Soaking	Placed in a running stream for several days.
Dried	In sun for 27–30 days (10 per cent maximum moisture).
Product	Chuño is consumed by soaking in water and then cooking in soups, or eaten with meat, cheese etc.
Advantages	Long storage life of up to four years. The process has the great advantage of not requiring fuel, a very scarce commodity in these high areas.
Disadvantages	Product dependent on climatic conditions (frost, cold running water, sun). Considerable loss of nutrients, particularly protein and vitamin C.

Product	Papa seca (Dried potato)
Region	South America
Country	Andean highlands in Peru and Bolivia.
Equipment	Cooking pot, tin sheet or sack.
Process	Essentially partial cooking followed by sun-drying.
Raw material	Potatoes
Preparation	Boiled and peeled by hand then sliced or broken into small pieces.
Dried	Sun-dried on tin sheets or sacks.
Product	The product is used in many traditional dishes.
Advantages	Useful method of utilizing smaller second grade potatoes. Has considerably more market acceptability than chuño; higher value product than chuño.
Disadvantages	Fuel is required for boiling.

Product	Potato starch
Region	South America
Country	Peru
Equipment	Grinder, large jars, cotton cloth.
Process	Pulping, washing and sun-drying.

Preparation	The potatoes are peeled.
Pulped	Ground into a pulp, thereby breaking down the cell walls and releasing the starch. The resulting milk contains mainly starch together with minor amounts of skin and fibre particles. If the latter are not removed by washing and sieving, a brown-coloured starch which has a lower market value will result.
Settling	The ground pulp is diluted with water and left to settle in large containers. The starch settles to the bottom. After the liquid above the starch has been poured off the starch is re-slurried in water and again allowed to settle. This washing process is repeated several times until a clean white product results.
Drained	The starch is drained by squeezing in a cotton cloth.
Dried	Placed in the sun to dry.

Note: Very little traditional starch processing is now carried out at household level, having largely been replaced by maize and potato starch imported from Europe and the USA.

Yam

Yams are an important staple food in West Africa, the Caribbean, parts of South-east Asia and the Pacific. In West Africa the yam 'zone' principally covers the Ivory Coast, Ghana, Togo, Benin and Nigeria with the last being the world's largest producer.

Traditionally, yams have an important cultural role. In the yam 'zone', it is commonly forbidden to eat the first yams of the new harvest until the annual New Yam Festival occurs. There is also a gender division associated with the handling of the crop. Generally, in West Africa and Melanesia, men control the growing and storing of the crop. Some women, especially widows, may grow and store yams. This is advantageous to women in West African communities where a well-built and stocked yam barn is considered prestigious. However, in Melanesia, the gender taboo is stronger, and women are excluded from all cultivation stages of one particular yam species (*Dioscorea alta*), but are allowed to cultivate other less important species. This particular species may have been designated the man's crop and attained ritual importance because of the high labour and financial investment required for its cultivation. Another cultural belief common in West Africa is that small tubered species are thought to produce an inferior 'fufu', and thus considered an inferior gift.

Yam is a more difficult and expensive crop to cultivate than cassava. Labour inputs and material costs are higher as not only does a yam crop require more husbandry but also greater soil fertility. It is a seasonal crop and part of a live tuber is required as planting material for the next season. Because of the perishable nature of the planting material the farmer does not necessarily have the next season's crop secured. This means that the producer requires a well managed store and may on occasions have to purchase suitable planting material from elsewhere.

Some varieties of yams will store for up to six months. There are well-developed traditional storage systems in the major yam-growing regions. These may involve leaving the tubers in the ground or heaping freshly harvested tubers underneath rock outcrops, on household floors, inside huts, underneath houses built on stilts or underneath soil and humus. Under these conditions the rate of deterioration is reduced by curing, which is described later under the relevant heading. In parts of West Africa special structures are built for the storage of tubers. These 'yam barns' consist of a vertical framework of timbers with cross pieces of bamboo or the ribs of palm leaves. Tubers are fastened individually to the structure using raffia.

Yams are usually prepared for eating using simple cooking such as boiling, baking, roasting, steaming or frying.

Throughout the West African yam zone fufu is the most popular processed yam product.

Certain varieties are preferred for fufu production as they form a stiffer dough. In the Pacific Islands yams are wrapped in green leaves with other ingredients such as coconut cream and chicken or fish and roasted in ovens.

Although there are about six hundred species of yams, only about ten are edible, and many contain toxic alkaloids. Some toxic varieties are traditionally processed as in the Philippines where, for example, the following technique is used:

o thin slices of peeled tuber are placed in a basket and submerged in the sea or a solution of salt water for two to three hours;
o the slices are removed and squeezed under weights for a few hours;
o the material is replaced in the basket and left in a running stream for 36–48 hours with occasional stirring.

Traditionally processed products

Fufu is one example of a range of sticky dough or porridge-like foods.

The name is often applied to any such product made from starchy material such as cassava, yam, cocoyam or plantain, either singly or in combination. It is also sometimes used to describe similar doughs made from cassava starch, cassava flour or grated cassava. Numerous local variations and methods of preparation thus occur. An excellent survey is included in the *Further Reading* list (Lancaster, *et al.*, 1982).

Traditionally processed products

Product	Fufu
Region	West Africa
Equipment	Pestle and mortar, sieve, raffia or cotton bags.
Process	Raw material pounded or mashed to make a heavy dough.
Raw material	Yam, cassava, cocoyam or plantain, or blends of these.
Preparation	Peeled and cut into smaller pieces (but see Note overleaf).
Cooked	Boiled or steamed till soft.
Pounded	In a pestle and mortar with a little water until a smooth, sticky dough forms, which is then ready for consumption.
Product	A heavy dough.

Note: The preparation of fufu from 'bitter' cassava will differ: unpeeled roots are placed in streams or in large earthenware pots for three to five days for soaking and fermenting. The roots soften and the peel and central fibres may then be removed, after which the product is ground or pounded in a mortar until a smooth soft mash results.

Product	Yam flour
Region	West Africa
Country	Togo, Ghana, Ivory Coast, Benin, Nigeria.
Equipment	Pestle and mortar, sieve, knive.
Preparation	Tubers are peeled and sliced to about 1cm thickness and parboiled in water.
Dried	After cooling, the pieces are sun-dried until hard. In this chip form, the product is referred to as 'elubo' in Nigeria.
Ground	Ground into coarse flour with pestle and mortar, although mills are used where available.
Sieved	To produce a finer flour. Grinding and sieving is repeated until product is satisfactory.
Advantages	Flour can be prepared from damaged tubers, thus limiting crop and storage losses. It can be stored for several months, provided that the moisture content is sufficiently low and the product is protected from insect and rodent attack.
	The dry chips can also be stored and ground to flour as required. This has the added advantage of giving greater stability to moisture absorption. A stable product allows for reduction in marketing and transport costs.
Disadvantages	Certain varieties of yam turn black or brown and can be extremely hard when dry. This has met with consumer resistance.
	'Elubo' is very hard and difficult to grind using conventional milling machines and causes machine wear.

Note: The flour can be rehydrated with water to form a dough as needed, but considered an inferior substitute for fufu.

Edible aroids

Aroids are physiologically similar to root crops, although they do not yield edible roots but swollen, starchy stems. They are cultivated, processed and consumed as a dietary staple in a similar way to root crops. Many aroids contain irritant crystals of oxalic acid and special cooking methods have been developed to make them safe and palatable. Within the edible aroid group, taro and tannia species are the main food crops used for direct human consumption. Tannia, taro and allied species are often collectively known as cocoyams.

Cocoyam cultivation and processing for direct consumption is a subsistence activity. Again, the crop requires high labour and material inputs compared with cassava.

Traditional processing methods are limited to boiling, mashing, drying and fermentation. Commercial production includes products such as weaning foods, flakes, breakfast foods, noodles, canned and frozen goods. Such activities which require cultivation to be on a larger scale are concentrated in Hawaii, the Philippines, the Caribbean islands and Egypt. Although taro and tannia appear similar, they have developed in different hemispheres. Both crops are important staples in West Africa, while in Oceania taro is preferred. Taro requires more careful processing than tannia to eliminate the larger amounts of oxalic acid present.

In West Africa, tannia is commonly boiled and pounded with other root crops into fufu, or eaten boiled, fried, or roasted. In Hawaii and southern China, taro is fermented to make a purplish-grey paste known as 'poi'.

Traditionally processed products

Product	Poi
Region	Pacific
Country	Hawaii
Equipment	Knife, grater, sieve.
Process	Cooking and grating.
Preparation	After cooking, taro is peeled, washed and grated.
Fermented	The resulting liquid mass is kept at ambient temperatures for several days to ferment, during which time lactic acid is produced.
Product	When fermentation has produced the desired taste, the poi is ready for eating.

Sweet potato

The sweet potato originated in Latin America and is now widely grown throughout tropical and sub-tropical regions, particularly in the Pacific, Caribbean, East Asia and New Zealand. It is not generally eaten as a main dietary staple in the same way as cassava, maize or rice; that is to say with almost every meal. The research that has been carried out on sweet potato is mainly in connection with processed products for the crop in the developed world. In the USA it is canned, frozen, dehydrated or used in pie fillings and baby foods. Sweet potatoes are comparatively easy to grow and have high consumer acceptability. However, they have a short storage life, generally less than four weeks in the tropics. Their thin skin is easily damaged during harvest and post-harvest handling leaving the crop highly perishable. They are therefore usually consumed soon after harvesting. Alternatively, curing, drying and fermentation are traditional preservation methods, some of which are described on the following page.

Traditionally processed products

Product	Chips
Region	East Africa, Asia (India)
Process	Slicing and drying.
Preparation	Tubers are peeled and sliced.
Dried	The pieces are placed in the sun to dry and can then be stored. When the product is needed for consumption, the dried slices are washed and boiled or ground into flour for making local dishes.

Product	Flakes
Region	South-east Asia
Country	Philippines
Process	Drying and pounding.
Preparation	The tubers are peeled and flaked.
Dried	Placed in the sun to dry and then stored. For consumption the dried flakes are pounded into a flour and either made into gruel by mixing with water and sugar, or formed into small balls of a dough consistency, wrapped in sugar cane leaves and boiled.

Product	Flour
Region	South America
Country	Peru
Process	Drying and milling.
Preparation	The tubers are peeled and sliced.
Dried	Placed in the sun to dry.
Milling	The dried slices are milled and sieved to produce a flour.

Product	Fermented sweet potato 'Poi'
Region	Asia
Process	The tubers are baked or steamed.
Preparation	After cooking, the tubers are peeled and pounded with a stone pestle in a long, shallow bowl of wood or stone.
Fermented	The sticky dough is mixed with water and left in a calabash to ferment for several days (depending on local tastes).

Product	Futali
Region	Africa
Country	Malawi
Process	Cooking and pounding.
Cooked	Boiled or roasted.
Preparation	Pounded together with peanuts to form a paste.

Cassava

The majority of the total world production of cassava is processed for direct human consumption in Africa and South America. In Asia, Thailand produces cassava chiefly for industrial purposes and export. Such industrial applications include animal feed, alcohol, starch and food products such as tapioca and 'instant' mixes.

Cassava processing is not only important for preservation of the product which, as has been mentioned, must be used quickly after harvesting but also to reduce its toxic components. The toxicity of cassava has been covered in Chapter 1.

Traditionally processed products

Product	Gari
Region	Africa
Country	Nigeria, Ghana
Equipment	Grater, roasting pan, sieve, jute or fibre bag.
Process	Fermentation and roasting.
Preparation	Washed, peeled and grated roots are placed in large cloth bag in the sun and left to ferment for three to four days. Weights are placed on top of the bag to press out the liquid which drains away.
Sieved	When sufficiently dry (about 50 per cent water content) the pulp is removed from the sack and sieved to remove fibrous material.
Roasted	Small amounts are constantly stirred in a shallow pan over heat until cooked. Palm oil is sometimes added to prevent burning and to impart a yellow colour.
Cooled	Spread out to dry further and cool.
Product	A light, crisp, free-flowing granular powder which is creamy-white in colour. Shelf-life: a few weeks or months to more than one year depending on packaging and moisture content. For safe storage, moisture content must be below 12 per cent.
	Also known as 'Farinha de mandioca' in Brazil which is somewhat different in that its fermentation and pressing times (because of the Tipiti press) are much shorter. The product also has a different taste.
Advantages	Usually eaten as a convenience food and is therefore attractive to urban markets. When packaged properly it has a good shelf-life.
Disadvantages	Grating and peeling are time-consuming; frequent cuts on the hands with hand-graters.
	Constant stirring of gari over a fire requires processor to endure heat and smoke and exposure to an atmosphere of cyanide gas for lengthy periods of time.

Product	Landang or Cassava rice
Region	Asia
Country	Philippines
Raw material	Cassava
Equipment	Grater, jute sacks, winnowing basket, sieve, mat.
Process	The following are two common methods used to prepare this traditional Philippine dish.

Method 1

Preparation	Freshly harvested roots are peeled, grated, and placed in jute sacks.
De-watered	The sacks are pressed between two wooden blocks to squeeze out the juice.
Pelleted	The pulp is put into winnowing baskets and whirled until pellets form (size depends on speed of motion and moisture content).
Sieving	Pellets of more or less uniform size are isolated by sifting — those too big to pass through the sieve are broken, put back in and whirled again.
Steamed	The pellets are steamed on a screen placed over a vat of boiling water.
Dried	After being separated by hand while still wet, the pellets are finally sun-dried on mats.

Method 2

Preparation	Peeled roots are soaked in water in earthenware jars or wooden containers (contact with metal should be avoided) until they begin to soften (five to seven days). The contents are macerated and fibres removed by hand. The mass is air-dried, before making the pellets as described before. In both methods the pellets are thoroughly sun-dried for three to five days before storage. The product can be eaten without further cooking, or can be soaked, mixed with coconut milk, reboiled and served.
Advantages	If placed in a cool, dry place, the storage life is three to six months. Considered ideal for fishermen and others on trips as it stores well and can be eaten without cooking.

Product	Gaplek (Cassava chips)
Region	South-east Asia
Country	Indonesia
Equipment	Jute mats
Process	Drying
Preparation	Peeled and cut into thin slices.
Dried	Spread on woven mats or hung on fences to sun-dry. The drying time varies with the amount of sunny weather, but it is normally two to three days. The chips are sometimes steamed before drying, which, it is reported, prolongs the storage life.

Product   Cassava chips are usually further processed as needed for consumption: boiled, fried in oil, or ground into flour.

Note: Preparation of cassava into dried chips followed by further processing into flour when needed is widely practised in Asia. In Thailand and Indonesia, cassava chip production is also carried out at the commercial level, being a primary export. In India the chips are parboiled before drying. Storage life can be up to one year compared to three to six months without parboiling. In Ghana, the smaller whole roots which might otherwise be discarded are peeled and left in the sun for approximately ten days to dry. This product is known as 'Kokonte'.

Product   Cassareep (West Indies)
                 Tucupy (Brazil)

Region   South America, West Indies

Equipment   Grater, press or 'Tipiti'.

Process   Extraction and concentration

Preparation   Roots are peeled and freshly grated.

De-watered   Pressed to obtain juice which is collected.

Evaporated   The liquid obtained is boiled down and concentrated by evaporation until it reaches a dark, syrupy consistency. The long heating destroys the toxins in the juice.

Product   A thick syrupy sauce.

Advantages   Long storage life

Note: Along the Caribbean coastal areas, cassareep is the basis of the traditional dish 'pepper pot' in which all kinds of meat, fish and vegetable leftovers from meals can be placed and cooked. Cassareep is said to be a meat-preserver and pepper pots can be kept for many years by adding further ingredients as necessary and bringing to the boil daily. Bitter varieties of cassava are considered to give the best quality cassareep.

Product   Cassabe. (This one example of the many types of cassava bread traditionally produced in many countries.)

Region   South America.

Country   Venezuela

Equipment   Tipiti press, sieve, iron plate or griddle, trays.

Process   Grating, drying and baking.

Preparation   Two methods are used depending upon whether the roots are subjected to a soaking fermentation stage or simply peeled and grated.

De-watered   The juice is squeezed out from the mash using a Tipiti. The resulting 'press cake' is left for several hours or overnight until it becomes quite solid.

Sieved   The cake is broken up and rubbed or sifted through a coarse sieve to separate out extraneous fibres.

Dried	The dough is pressed down to a thickness of 1cm in wide trays made of woven palm fibre and left in the sun until completely dry and hard.
Baked	The press cake is either sun-baked or baked over a fire. Alternatively, the sifted pulp is spread into thin flat cakes and cooked on a hot griddle, turning to cook both sides to produce a hard cake. The cakes are then dried in the sun on the roofs of houses until they become hard. The cakes so produced can be two to three feet in diameter; pieces are broken off and dipped in gravy and soups.
Advantages	The hard brittle cake keeps in good condition for easy storage for several months, a convenient food to carry on extended trips, such as when hunting.
Disadvantages	A laborious process which can take up to two days.

Note: Cassabe or cassava bread is the staple diet of the Amazonian Indians. Bitter cassava is preferred as it has a higher starch content which makes the product less brittle and better to store.

Product	Cassava beer
Region	Widespread, including Central and East Africa and Latin America.
Equipment	Earthenware jars
Process	Kasiri is one example of a common fermented alcoholic beverage based on cassava.
Method 1	
Preparation	Fresh tubers are left up to a week in a flowing stream until detoxified by fermentation.
Fermented	The fermented cassava is removed from the stream, put into a jar and water is added. It is left to stand for another three days after which the mass is heated. In some cases yeast is then added before allowing the fermentation to continue.
Method 2	
Preparation	This process is widely used throughout Central and South America, and the West Indies. Cassava bread is chewed up, mixed with water, and fermented for two to three days. The natural enzymes of the saliva speed up fermentation by initiating the breakdown of starch to sugar. Traditional customs require that only young girls chew the cassava in some areas while only the oldest women are permitted to do so in others. Without chewing, fermentation takes four to five days.
	The drink has ritual importance for some tribes in the Brazilian tropical forest.

Product	Starch
Region	South Pacific
Country	Tonga and Western Samoa
Equipment	Knife, bucket, grater, strainer, mats

Process	Extraction, drying
Preparation	Fresh roots are washed, peeled and grated into coarse meal.
Extracted	Grated cassava is washed with water, strained through a cloth bag which is squeezed by hand to extract starch milk. This is then poured into a bucket or basin. The process is repeated until the squeezed liquid is no longer white.
Decanted	After standing for several hours the starch will settle to the bottom.
Washed	The starch is washed and the procedure repeated until the liquid poured off is clear.
Dried	The white starch remaining at the bottom of the basin is removed and spread out on mats to dry in the sun.
Product	When almost dry it is either pressed into balls or dried completely and pounded into powder.

Note: Traditionally, starch was made from arrowroot, or sago palm. Since cassava is cheaper it has tended to replace these starches. The most common use is to add to puddings or mix with fruit. Cassava starch can be stored as needed. It is baked into cakes in the Caribbean, Pacific Islands and Jamaica. Cassava starch can be further processed into tapioca: wet starch is heated in a pan, stirring continuously until the grains burst and gelatinize into globules. In West Africa, starch is traditionally processed, dried, rehydrated later and eaten as pap or porridge.

Traditional curing methods

The purpose of curing is to increase the storage life of the tuber. During curing, conditions of increased temperature and humidity encourage growth of the outer layers of the tuber's skin. Existing wounds are thus sealed, preventing entry of micro-organisms and thereby helping to inhibit deterioration. Curing is practised with cassava, sweet potato and especially with yams.

In Papua New Guinea the tubers are stacked on platforms in a dark area of the house where heat and humidity from the cooking area can cure them. On the other hand, the Maoris of New Zealand practise pit storage as a method of curing sweet potatoes. Here, underground storage pits are dug into the side of a hill and the floor of the pit is covered with a layer of gravel and soft packing. The seed stock is placed in first to fill the back of the pit, while the tubers for consumption are stacked at the front, being separated by fern leaves. The store is sealed to allow a build-up of heat and humidity inside for curing (owing to the natural respiration of the tubers).

Pit storage is also practised in Zimbabwe and Malawi. Yams are usually cured by covering the tubers with earth.

3

Improved processing equipment and products

MANY OF THE traditional processing systems outlined in the previous section have been improved and in many cases mechanized.

When considering upgrading traditional methods or introducing improved technologies, it is important to be sure that:

○ the need is correctly identified
○ appropriate expertise (including technical, socio-economic, and marketing) is available.

The introduction of improved technologies for root crop processing has met with varying degrees of success. Mechanical peelers, for example, have in some cases resulted in higher wastage than hand peeling and in general have not proved acceptable in small processing units. Graters on the other hand seem to have met with wider acceptance, being able to take over what is seen as a very laborious task.

Complete 'packages' of equipment, of various scales, are available for processing several root crops. Comparatively small packages exist, for example, for carrying out all the process steps in the production of gari and secondary cassava products such as chips, instant mixes and breakfast foods. Some of these products are not part of traditional local foods and are too expensive for most villagers. They therefore have little or no readily available rural market.

Most small rural villages do not have the facilities to meet the necessary requirements of high capital investment; a regular and formal labour force; access to and a regular supply of production materials, and management abilities necessary to operate larger-scale plants. For this reason package systems available will not be covered in this text. There appear to be few, if any, cottage or small-scale mechanized 'packages' for processing a particular root crop.

This chapter describes improved technologies for processing and includes:

○ Peeling and washing
○ Grating and rasping
○ Pounding
○ Pressing and de-watering
○ Sieving
○ Roasting
○ Drying
○ Milling and grinding .
○ Chipping and slicing

As it is not known which pieces of equipment used in these processes are still prototypes, have been tested in the field, or are actually being used by rural women at village level, the names and addresses of the equipment suppliers and appropriate institutions are given at the end of the book as a first contact point. It should be stressed that before considering obtaining any equipment it would be beneficial to consult appropriate institutions, especially those who have had previous experience of introducing the equipment.

The introduction of an improved technology or process may benefit a community both economically and socially. Increasing the efficiency of a process by making it more cost-effective with the aim of increasing incomes will also result in social change, which will have to be acceptable to those involved. Both economic and social factors therefore need to be considered.

Economic factors

o Availability of local workshop facilities to produce or maintain the improved production system.
o Labour requirements and availability.
o Raw material supply.
o Scale of production desired.
o Production and product cost. The product may have to compete economically with traditional products made using unpaid or low-cost family labour.
o Potential consumer markets.
o Access to credit at local interest rates.

Social factors

o Family needs and capacity for labour and/or capital investments.
o Existing infrastructural support, i.e. transport and credit conditions.
o Cultural restrictions — gender divisions, local preferences in taste, texture, colour and odòur of food, taboos, social structures.

Consumer acceptability is vital for a food processing operation to market its products. It is necessary then to examine and compare any change in terms of flavour, colour, texture and odour that might have occurred with the introduction of an improved technology.

Peeling and washing

While equipment for washing and peeling root crops is commercially available its cost and throughput is generally too high for small rural projects.

Washing machines generally consist of a cylinder fitted with paddles and brushes that can be rotated while a stream of water is played over the root crop as it passes through the unit.

Mechanical peelers operate by rubbing the roots against a rotating abrasive surface. They are best suited to raw materials of regular shape. Irregular materials either have high losses on peeling or require final hand-peeling. The use of mechanical peelers is dependent on the throughput required and local wage rates. In Europe, with its high hourly labour costs for example, the cost of hand-peeling would far exceed any losses of yield through mechanical peeling. It should be noted that in some cases abrasive peelers may offer a reduction in losses compared to hand-peeling, especially when used for small roots or tubers.

A description of a simple washer and peeler that could be constructed locally together with a commercial peeler are included, together with an outline of a chemical peeling process.

CIP Manual potato washer

The International Potato Centre (CIP) in Peru has designed a simple, hand-operated potato washer. A 250-litre (55-gallon) oil drum is cut lengthwise and paddle wheels equipped with brushes are fixed onto an axle with wooden dowels. A handle is fixed to the axle in order to rotate the paddles and so agitate the potatoes. The washer has a capacity of 25kg of potatoes and requires 150 litres of water per batch. After a few minutes the drum is turned on its side to empty the potatoes and dirty water.

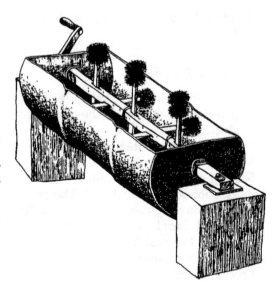

CIP Belt-driven motorized peeler

A sheet-metal cylinder or 250-litre drum, whose surface has been punched from the outside to create an abrasive surface internally, is mounted on a horizontal axle. The drum is rotated via a belt-drive from a motor. Potatoes are fed into the drum from the top, and as the cylinder rotates the protruding holes scrape the skin from the surface of the potatoes. Each end of the cylinder is fitted with a small door so that the potatoes may enter at one end and leave from the other when peeling is complete. A perforated metal pipe set above the cylinder sprays water over the rotating drum. 20kg of potatoes can be peeled in four minutes. Final trimming and peeling is necessary. A smaller hand-operated peeler can be constructed using a similar design.

Abrasive plate peeler

The 'Crypto Peerless' abrasive drum peeler is an example of a typical commercial machine in which a rotating abrasive drum rubs the skin from the material passed through. It is most commonly used to peel potatoes. Various sizes of such machines are available from as small as 13kg/batch. They are powered by electric motors.

Lye peeling

Hot solutions of sodium hydroxide (lye) can be used to loosen skin of many root crops to facilitate later peeling, such as removal by water spray or scrubbing with brushes. A combination of chemical reaction and heat softens and loosens the skin. The desired effect can be obtained by selecting the combination of lye concentration, temperature and immersion time.

Technical advice should be sought if lye peeling is being considered, as problems can occur. For example, partial cooking and gelatinization of the outer layers of the root may cause too much lye absorption. In addition, sodium hydroxide is a very dangerous chemical to handle and workers need to be properly trained and protected. In addition, the used lye solution is a potential source of pollution and can corrode equipment. Table 3 shows suitable combinations found for the lye peeling of yam.

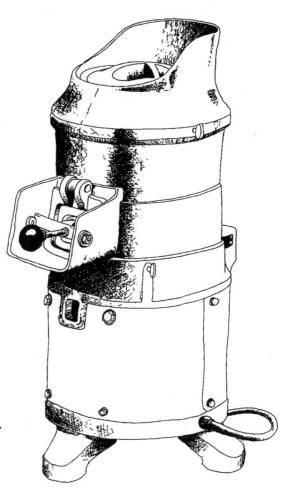

Table 3. Relation between immersion time and lye concentration on the efficiency of the lye peeling operation

Lye concentration (% by weight)	Time of immersion (minutes)	Visual evaluation[1]	Loss in weight of lye-peeled tubers[2] (%)
10	2	Questionable	5.60
	3	Questionable	11.11
	4	Questionable	12.78
	5	Good	14.44
	6	Very good	17.50
15	2	Questionable	7.22
	3	Questionable	11.11
	4	Good	13.33
	5	Very good	16.11
20	1	Questionable	6.67
	2	Questionable	8.89
	3	Good	12.21
	4	Very good	13.33

1 *Questionable:* Tubers retained large patches of peel or many small patches.
  Good: Tubers with one or two small patches of peel which can be removed easily by trimming.
  Very good: Tubers completely peeled.
2 Average of three runs.

Source: Rivera-Ortiz and Gonzales, 1972.

Grating and rasping

Grating and rasping are common steps in the processing of cassava and are time-consuming and hard work. A considerable number of graters exist which range from simple hand-graters through pedal operated units to motorized versions. Many are based on a rotating horizontal disc or vertical drum grating surface against which the root is held. Care should be taken when introducing any powered device that injuries do not occur: for example loose clothing becoming tangled in the drive, or fingers being caught in the rotating disc.

Hand-graters

The two designs of hand-graters shown here are both low-cost and can be constructed of tin or galvanized mild steel. The grating surface is created by puncturing the surface with holes, as in traditional construction. Both models need only one operator and are probably most suitable for an individual family or to be shared among a few families.

This design is essentially an upgraded traditional technology, with the grating surface horizontal instead of at a downward slant, often supported against the processor's legs. The elevated grater is now supported on a table.

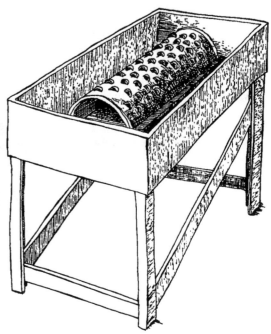

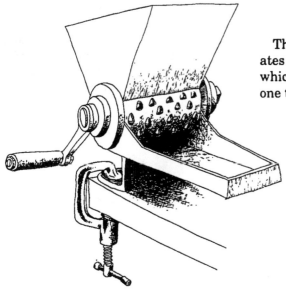

This hand-operated machine incorporates a rotating cylindrical grater against which the root is pressed. Note that only one tuber can be inserted at a time.

Pedal-operated cassava grater

In the early 1970s, an engineer at the
Intermediate Technology Development
Group's workshop in Zaria, Nigeria,
developed a cassava grater made from
galvanized iron tubing, spare bicycle
parts, hacksaw blades and sheet metal.
Cassava is fed in the hopper and a vertical disc with grating slits fixed to a frame
is rotated by pedal power.

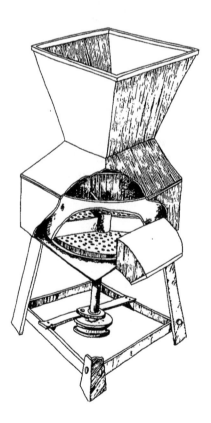

Wadwha disc grater

This grater, developed in Ghana, consists
of a disc-shaped wooden block to which a
perforated metal sheet is nailed. The perforated disc is rotated by a belt drive from
a 5hp diesel engine. The throughput is
one tonne of cassava per hour.

Vertical drum grater

This drum grater was developed by TAEC (Tikonko Agricultural Extension Centre) in Sierra Leone. The surface of the drum is covered with a sheet of perforated metal which rotates across the base of the feed hopper. The cassava is pressed against the grating surface by a wooden block inserted in the throat of the hopper. The drum is rotated by belt drive from a 4hp diesel or electric motor. The hopper, drum, and frame can be made from timber or scrap metal.

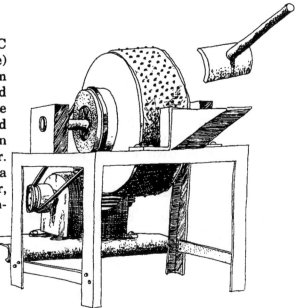

Pounding

The pounding of fufu from yams and cassava to produce a gelatinous, sticky product can take up to one hour using a traditional pestle and mortar.

Attempts to produce pounded yam products by rehydrating yam flour have proved unpopular because both the texture and taste were inferior to those of traditionally pounded yam.

Motorized pounding machine

A machine for pounding yams and similar foods has been developed at the Department of Agricultural Engineering, University of Ife in Nigeria. It consists of a beater and bowl which operate in a manner rather similar to a heavy dough mixer. The leading edge of the beater is sharpened to provide an additional chopping effect, with further beating producing a soft consistency characteristic of pounded foods. As in the traditional process, water is added as necessary during the process. The unit is powered by a 1.75hp motor and can produce enough fufu for eight adults in 45 seconds.

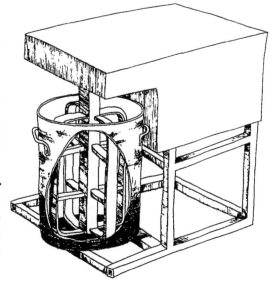

Pressing and de-watering

The common pressing step that occurs in several traditional root crop processing systems can remove up to 50 per cent of the water present. Several press designs exist ranging from the simple, easily constructed parallel press board, press frame or wedge press to more sophisticated screw and hydraulic presses. The latter clearly require access to better equipped workshops.

Upgraded traditional press

The traditional sticks-and-rope press has been upgraded by the Tikonko Agricultural Extension Centre in Sierra Leone. Two wooden frames are placed below and above the sacks filled with cassava mash. Six threaded rods pass through the bottom frame to fit holes in the top frame. Tightening exerts pressure on the sacks by pressing the frame closer together. The actual pressing time is not reduced but rather the time and labour necessary either to gather and heap heavy stones or to assemble and tie up the sticks around the sacks is reduced. Only wood, bolts and threaded rods are needed.

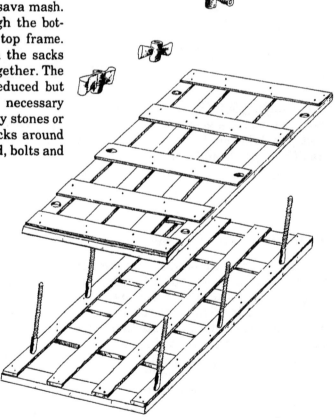

TCC Parallel board press

The Technology Consultancy Centre
(TCC) in Ghana has developed a parallel
board press which provides uniform
pressure to pulp-filled sacks placed between them. Instead of a wooden frame as
in the TAEC upgraded traditional model,
two solid parallel boards are screwed together to create the pressure on the sacks.
It takes about three to four hours to de-
water one bag (125kg) of gari as opposed
to three to four days needed by traditional
presses.

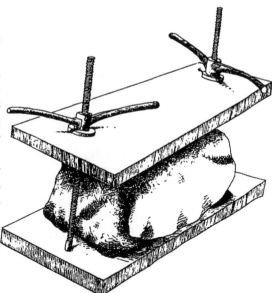

Wedge press

The wedge press is an adaptation of a
traditional Chinese press used to extract
oil.

Tree stumps or wooden logs provide
support for a wooden beam inserted in
between them. Sacks of grated pulp are
placed on the beam and pressure is applied when wooden wedges are hammered
into the space between the sacks and tree
stump.

Screw press

Screw-type cassava presses can be in the form of either a circular press cage holding the fresh pulp or a square frame exerting pressure on the sacks. Both types illustrated here work by moving a heavy circular or square block which is lowered or raised by means of a threaded shaft. The press cage has a capacity of approximately one bag (125kg) of cassava per batch, whereas the other design can handle several sacks of pulp. A lathe is needed for cutting the screw thread, as well as metal bending and cutting equipment.

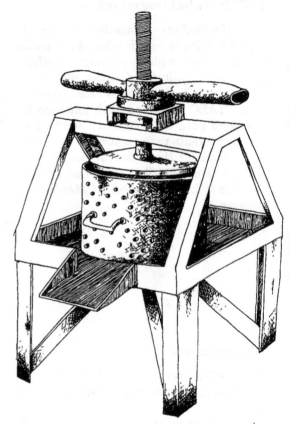

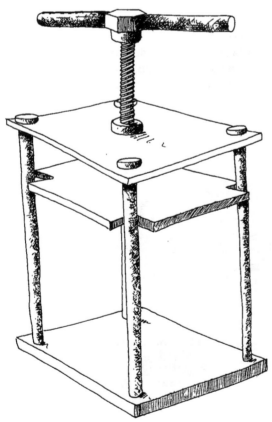

Hydraulic press

Some designs of press use a hydraulic car or lorry jack to apply pressure to the material being de-watered, usually between pressing boards. If discarded car jacks are not available, the imported jack can make it an expensive piece of machinery to produce and maintain. Care is needed to prevent leakage of poisonous hydraulic fluid.

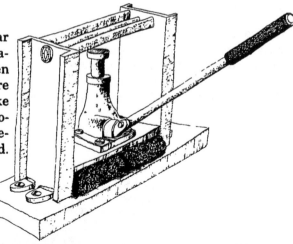

Sieving

After the pulp is de-watered by pressing, the residual cake is traditionally broken up by manually rubbing it against wire mesh or raffia sieves. This process can be mechanized using either a vibrating or rotating sieve.

Improved pulverizer and sifter

At the University of Nigeria a prototype sieve unit has been developed which cuts up the cake into small pieces which then pass on a conveyor belt to a vibratory sieve. Output is 125kg per hour.

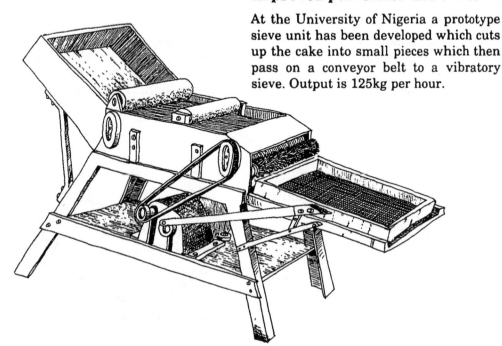

Rotating drum sieve

Agrico Ltd in Ghana have developed a unit made from a 200-litre (44-gallon drum) fitted with a cylindrical sieve made of wire netting. The cake enters through a hopper and is then sifted when the drum is rotated, exiting from the bottom. A power-operated version has been developed by the same company which is driven by belt drive from a small motor.

Roasting

Gari is traditionally heated in shallow cast-iron pans over a fire while being pressed and stirred against the hot surface with calabash pieces to prevent burning. Improvements have included either upgrading the traditional pan and wooden stirrer or the development of a rotating cylindrical roasting drum.

Upgraded gari roaster

One example is a rectangular tray roaster developed by the Rural Agro-Industrial Development Scheme in Nigeria. A chimney helps to draw air which reduces the effects of smoke and heat on the processor. A long wooden stirrer or rake is used to turn the cake, preventing it from sticking and burning. This upgraded system protects the operator's health because the smoke is channelled away from the processor and the long stirrer allows her to remain some distance from the fire.

Cylindrical roaster

Agrico in Ghana have developed a prototype cylindrical roaster containing paddles which continuously stir the gari as the drum is heated. It can be hand- or mechanically-driven and heated by either wood or gas.

Drying

Technology choices exist for drying root crop products ranging from basic traditional systems which could consist of hanging the material from sticks, right through to forced air driers. We have already seen, under gari roasting, one traditional method of drying. This section will cover drying devices in the more accepted sense and include examples of solar, kiln-type and forced air driers in order of increasing sophistication, expense and drying capacity. Although these represent the range of drying technologies available, they have not been widely used for root crops. Root crops and their products are of fairly low value and it is doubtful that the use of artificial driers would be economic, unless specialist consumer markets exist requiring dry products with considerable value added, e.g. potato crisps or other snack foods.

Solar drier

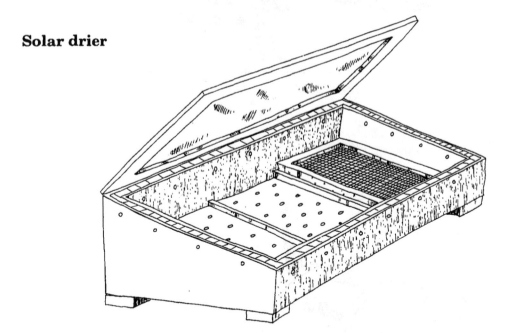

Simple solar driers glazed with a transparent top and a system of air vents located in the bottom and along the top of the sides are often referred to as Brace driers. The air in the chamber is heated by the sunlight passing through the transparent lid. The heated air rises and exits at the top of the drier, at the same time carrying away moisture from the product. An air flow develops with fresh air entering through the lower vents.

While these Brace driers are comparatively cheap and have been tried in many situations around the world, they do not seem to have achieved wide acceptability.

Kiln-type drier

Two designs of simple wood-fired driers are shown. In the first, sometimes known as a Brook Drier, a large tray is supported on a block or mudbrick base which has air entry holes in its sides. A flue passes under the tray through which hot air flows from a firebox to a chimney. Air entering the side vents is heated by passing over the flue. The McDowell drier is similar except that a transparent tent-like roof structure above the tray allows solar drying to be used when appropriate.

Milling and grinding

Lumps often occur in gari if the heat is not distributed evenly during roasting. These large lumps will remain after traditional sieving process and are normally sold as animal feed. In order to reduce waste (losses of up to 10 per cent can occur), roasted cassava can be milled in a conventional corn mill or hammer mill to reduce the lumps to a finer grade. Examples of hammer mills and plate mills are shown below.

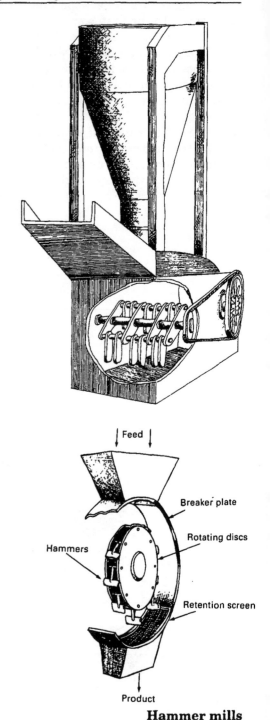

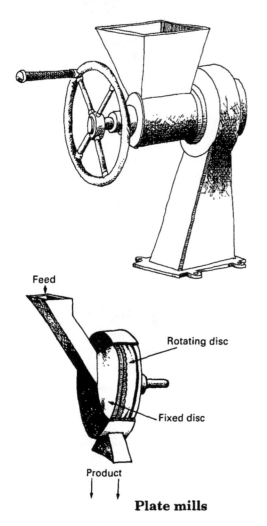

Plate mills

Hammer mills

Chipping and slicing

Slicing of root crops before drying reduces the drying time by exposing more surface area to the air. Slicing is also of course an important step prior to cooking root crops as it allows more rapid and even heat penetration.

Root crop slicer

The Department of Agricultural Chemistry and Food Science (DAC-FS) in the Philippines has designed a simple slicer which is said to cut sweet potatoes much faster than manual methods. The sweet potato is held on the cutting platform against a plate which controls the thickness of slice. Slices are then cut off with the hinged cutting blade. Capacity is 21–23kg (50lb) per hour.

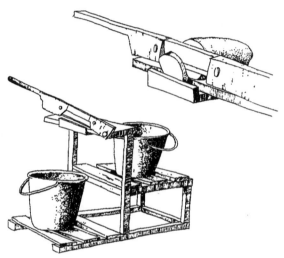

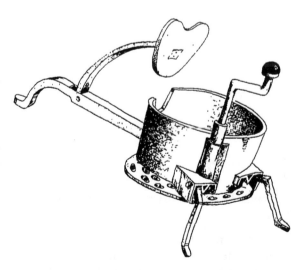

Hand-operated potato cutter

The International Potato Centre (CIP) has designed a cutter which consists of a horizontal rotating cutting disc. The potato is pressed down against the disc with one hand while the other hand turns a handle thus rotating the disc. This machine has been modified for motor drive with the disc running in a vertical plane. Cutting discs can be changed to alter cutting thicknesses if required. Crypto Peerless (whose address is listed) supply a similar motorized machine with capacities up to 270kg (600lb) per hour which slices, dices, chips, grates and shreds.

Root cutter

Nardi Francesco and Figli of Italy produce a manually operated root-chopper
containing a rotating disc fitted with four
blades.

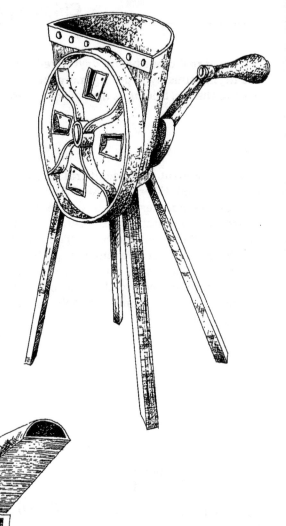

Pedal-operated cassava slicer

P.T. Kerta Laksana of Indonesia has
made a pedal-driven cassava slicer fitted
with one large slicing blade. It is claimed
to have a capacity of up to 500kg (1100lb)
per hour.

Table 4 outlines a comparison of traditional and improved technologies for gari
processing.

Table 4. A comparison of three technologies for the production of gari

Stage	Traditional labour-intensive	Post-traditional intermediate	Modern fully-mechanized
1. Raw material production and supply	Smallholder production Yield: c.10t/hectare/years	Smallholder production Yield: c.10t/hectare/years	Factory plantation and/or smallholder co-operative Yield: c.10–25t/hectare/years
	From traders	From traders	From purchasing agents on factory plantations
2. Peeling and washing	Manual: 38kg/hour; 25% raw material loss	Manual: 38kg/hour; 25% raw material loss	Mechanical abrasive peeler; 30% raw material loss
3. Size reduction	Manual: 23kg/hour Mechanical: 200kg/hour	Manual: 23kg/hour Mechanical: 200kg/hour	Mechanical: hammer mill (imported), 1500kg/hour
4. Fermentation	Fermentation and de-watering in heavily-weighted cloth or nylon bags	Batch fermentation in (aluminium) tanks	Batch fermentation in (aluminium) tanks
5. De-watering	See 4 above	Semi-mechanized: locally made hydraulic or mechanical press	Mechanized: hydraulic press
6. Screening	Manual: woven fibre screen	Semi-mechanized: locally made screen with hand- or mechanically driven paddle	Mechanized: motorized rotary screen
7. Garification	Manual; cast-iron pan over wood fire (combined stage with drying): 2.2kg/hour	Semi-mechanized: locally made wood-burning fryer (combined stage with drying): 70kg/hour	Mechanized: rotary kiln heated by oil burners 450kg/hour

[continued over]

Table 4. continued

Stage	Traditional labour-intensive	Post-traditional intermediate	Modern fully-mechanized
8. Drying	See 7 above	See above	Mechanized: rotary drum drier
9. Milling and sieving	Milling: not necessary Sieving: locally made	Milling: not required Sieving: vibrating hand or mechanical sieve	Milling: disc mill Sieving: vibrating multi-deck sieve
10. Packaging	50kg jute sacks	50kg heat sealed polyethylene bags	50kg heat sealed polyethylene bags
11. Material handling (all stages)	Manual	Manual, with trolleys	Belt conveyors, bucket elevators with trolleys
12. Marketing and distribution	Through traditional gari trade system in local markets	Through traditional trade system and supermarkets	Through traditional trade system and supermarkets
13. Purchasers	All income groups, rural and urban	Mainly urban higher income groups and institutions (e.g. schools, army)	Mainly urban higher income groups and institutions (e.g. schools, army)
14. Buildings	600m²	200m²	650m²
15. Employees per shift total unskilled	234 229 Predominantly female	45 40	28 9 Predominantly male

Source: Bruinsma *et al.* (1983)

4
Case studies

TRADITIONALLY, THE PROCESSING of root crops uses simple tools and methods, is highly labour-intensive and has low labour productivity. It is not surprising that time, therefore, is a major constraint for women practising traditional technologies.

These case studies illustrate a number of the problems that can arise when trying to upgrade these traditional activities.

The case study from Sierra Leone illustrates that one must consider the entire system, from cultivation to processing, before attempting to introduce improvements at any one stage in the process.

A common problem arising in technology dissemination is that men often have more access to cash activities in rural communities than women. Unless a credit scheme is provided with the technology, its high purchase cost will provide an effective constraint on women gaining any benefit. The case study from Ghana introducing gari-processing technology provides an example of this.

Mechanization can displace women from traditional income-earning activities. In Sierra Leone, the gari grater provided such an attractive new income source that the women's group lost control over the operation of the machine to the traditional village leader. This case study illustrates how vital it is to investigate the socio-political structures operating in a community when planning a project.

When considering ways to improve processing activities not only must the complex socio-economic environment be examined but also the infrastructure that may be needed to support the availability and diffusion of improved technologies for women.

The case studies in this chapter seek to provide an overview of the experiences gained in introducing improved root crop processing technologies.

Due to the lack of documentation on the impact of projects introducing different kinds of root crops and technologies, the case studies primarily cover cassava processing where the often high returns to gari production have encouraged technology innovation.

A case study from Papua New Guinea has been included which describes a sago palm processing project. Although sago palm is not a root crop, it is included because its lessons can be applied to many root crop processing activities. It shows clearly that introducing a new technology is not always necessary: transferring a traditional process from one area to another can work well given the availability of raw materials and markets.

Diesel-powered cassava grater, Sierra Leone

The Women's Programme of the Bo-Pujehun Rural Development Project operating in the Southern province of Sierra Leone introduced diesel-powered cassava graters on a pilot basis to selected villages beginning in 1984. The vertical drum graters were built locally at the Tikonko Agricultural Extension Centre (TAEC) in Bo, using timber and scrap metal. The 4hp diesel engines were imported from Germany and represented the most expensive part of the machine. Gari processing is a highly profitable activity. In times of rice shortage (the staple food) and for urban populations which are dependent on village farms for their supplies of rice, gari is a popular food. Gari has a high value compared to fresh cassava because it has a considerably longer storage life and transport costs are a small proportion of the value of the final product.

In a pre-feasibility study conducted in Bo town in 1984 by the project, it was seen that 23 per cent of the gari producers in the area were men. Normally, gari processing is considered women's activity in rural villages and such a high percentage of men was seen to result from the product's high profitability and the availability of improved technology in town centres.

Cassava processing in towns is usually done by hired motor-driven graters. Investment in a motor grater for the sole purpose of hiring it out is common. Given the domination of gari processing by women, it is ironic that only a small minority of women producers are owners of motorized graters.

This pattern of imbalance has been addressed by the Women's Programme by designing projects to improve women's access to improved technology, especially in the rural areas. A pilot project was initiated whereby motorized graters were introduced in a co-operative ownership basis in rural areas. A revolving fund was set up by the Women's Programme at a national bank whereby women's groups could get loans with flexible repayments. The purchase price of the grater was also subsidized by the project.

The revolving fund system allowed village women greater access to formal banks in that the collateral of project funds caused women to be seen as less risky borrowers to bank officials. In addition it gave the women an opportunity to learn about formal lending systems normally outside their experience. The flexibility of the payment schedule was adjusted to the seasonality of cassava production and the processors' other competitive labour obligations on the farm. This unique scheduling took into account the women's needs and was designed on a group by group basis.

The profitability of cassava products has led some farmers to shift production decisions in favour of cassava planting. In some villages located near to main roads allowing easy access to the capital city, almost the entire farm area was cropped with cassava and villagers used the proceeds from the sale of gari to buy rice and other staple foods. These changes have led to concerns over land being taken away from rice production in some areas and a general reduction of women's access to land for growing traditional food crops.

This interest in cassava has also led farmers to seek improved varieties. The women processors complained that the introduction of larger rooted improved cassava varieties with high water content resulted in an increased demand for fuelwood and subsequent processing time. Here is an example where the labour demands at different stages in the production cycle from cultivation to processed product were not taken into account by project planners and research stations. Although this particular variety was higher yielding and therefore more productive at the cultivation stage, labour demands were increased at the processing stage as a result of its introduction.

Another environmental factor which affected the pilot groups was that competing development agencies operating on different terms were working in the same areas. This caused great confusion for villagers seeking access to the grater technology as the graters were offered at different subsidized rates and in one instance were given out free, thereby discouraging self-sufficiency. One solution to this problem was that project managers met together and agreed on areas of operation.

Co-operation of group members was seen as critical to the success of the project. Before a loan could be applied for, adequate cropping areas of cassava had to be provided. In some cases this meant women farmers agreeing to put together their individual land holdings. In other cases it meant that the women in a village would organize a group together, request a piece of land from the chief, and agree to a communal work day each week on this land outside their individual household obligations.

Once the grater was set up and in operation, decisions had to be taken on a group basis regarding new members who wanted to join or old members who wanted to leave and needed compensation. Other issues which arose included: on what terms members and non-members could have access to the machine; what penalties would be enforced for those not coming to group meetings, communal work days, or contributing membership dues/in-kind payments towards the loan. Such co-operation requires relatively high management capabilities within the group. It was observed that the profitability of gari resulted in women processors leaving cassava cultivation in some villages, as it was recognized as a new cash crop for their men. In such cases, these women returned to more intense cultivation of vegetables for their income source.

In other instances cassava cultivation was turned into a 'joint activity' with men controlling the proceeds. Women without husbands would cultivate cassava alone, that is if they had the cash resources to hire labour. In this area married women were usually not allowed to keep separate cassava farms; it had to be a joint activity. Men feared such independence would put

women in a position to pay back their dowry and leave them.

The Women's Programme reviewed pilot villages in 1986 where graters had been installed. At least two of the orignal six were removed as the original owners had lost control of the machine. In one village the chief had designated his son to be the sole operator who would hire out the machine to neighbouring villages. (Bo-Pujehun Rural Development Project, 1986, and Bo-Pujehun Agricultural Programme, 1984)

Co-operative management of gari processing project, Ghana

Two pilot projects in Antoa and Damongo regions of northern Ghana were initiated under the guidance of the National Council on Women and Development (NCWD). Improved gari processing equipment consisting of a cassava grater, cassava press, gari roaster, and a milling machine were installed. There were several reasons for locating the project at these sites. The proximity to Kumasi offered easy marketability. The area was already an important cassava producing region and thus offered employment for women engaged in the industry.

Both the NCWD regional representative and the village chief encouraged the women to organize themselves. The chief provided support by allocating land for a project site.

The original group consisted of fourteen women and one man. All the women processed cassava into gari as a secondary occupation. Their primary activities included farming, selling cooked foods, making clothes and hiring out their labour to other farms.

Group members did not pay dues. They obtained the initial working capital from the Town Development Committee in order to purchase inputs such as sacks, metal basins, roasting pans and cassava. This loan has since been repaid.

Raw materials come from a variety of sources: purchased from other farms, harvested from group members' farms and the group-owned ten-acre farm.

The collection of firewood, harvesting, peeling, grating, roasting and bagging are done collectively as a group work effort. The gari is marketed in local villages and schools.

Group members have not shared the profits from sales amongst themselves but have chosen to use the funds to buy additional equipment. They feel they have benefited from co-operative management in that they have received some of the product to supplement their families' diets. The group has expressed an interest in increasing the membership. Since many of the tasks require physical strength, they would like more men to join the group.

Several villagers had applied to join the group but the NCWD regional secretary insisted on limiting the number. Some disgruntled villagers complained that the co-operative had limited membership in order to be exclusive.

Clearly, the members feel they have benefited from pooling their labour resources. The husbands of the female members were happy about the project's existence in that they felt it reduced financial responsibilities at home. (ILO/ NCWD, 1987)

Improved gari processing technologies, Nigeria

This case study is concerned with the introduction of improved gari processing technologies at an intermediate and in-dustrial scale. In selected rural villages in Bendel State, where the processing and sale of gari is a predominant income source for women, the introduction of such technologies has had a profound effect on their income.

Traditionally, the ploughing, planting and weeding of cassava farms is done by men. There are few women who cultivate their own farms. More often, women buy the unharvested tubers from men and harvest the tubers themselves. The peeling and grating of cassava is done by hand. Gari processing provides the main source of income for women in this area.

Diesel engine powered mechanical graters and hydraulic de-watering presses have replaced hand-grating methods and reduced the time needed for pressing. The high purchase cost of these technologies has resulted in only men owning and operating these machines. All the men belonged to a union which fixed prices for operations and organized work schedules for members. These work schedules were determined by the number of machines available in any village and the length of market days. Such a system was intended to avoid conflicts and disagreements over individual economic gains.

The mechanical grater and press introduced at village level increased gari productivity. The time needed for grating, considered one of the most laborious steps in the process, was greatly reduced. The de-watering step, which normally took five to eight days, was reduced to half an hour.

The introduction of the gari processing machinery also resulted in several adverse effects for the women in these areas. With the introduction of mechanical graters and presses, work traditionally done by women became the work of men. This transfer of control resulted in a transfer of income. Women lost an important income source. A set of four gari processing machines produced by a private Nigerian company were installed in one village in Bendel State. The system consisted of a cassava grater, dough sifter, mechanical press and garifier. Another component of the system, the peeler, was not bought.

The factory employed 48 workers to operate the machinery. Eleven of these were women whose tasks were to hand peel the cassava tubers and keep the factory clean. Gari produced from this factory was of very high quality and was only sold in the urban markets in places like Lagos and Ondo.

The sophisticated technology used by the factory was capable of producing very high quality gari. The garifier had a dual purpose of toasting as well as drying; heat supply could be regulated. The cylindrical machine fitted with prodders for stirring enabled the operator to avoid burns and eliminate contact with steam during stirring. It is interesting to note that the operations in the factory which were mechanized employed only male labour.

Female labour was minimal and was employed for a step in the process which was not mechanized. Women were employed for this work because available peeling machines in Nigeria were seen to be ineffective and women's labour was less costly.

From these experiences in Bendel State, it can be seen that the introduction of improved gari processing technologies were more beneficial to the men in the area than the women. At an intermediate level, the high capital cost of the machinery made it unavailable to the women while at the same time pushing them out of this economic activity altogether. (Williams, 1982)

Transfer of traditional technologies, Papua New Guinea

Although sago is not a root crop, it plays a similar role to root crops in the diets of people in Papua New Guinea. Processed sago serves as an important starch-based carbohydrate.

The Appropriate Technology Development Institute undertook a sago product development programme in order to re-establish sago as a valuable resource, develop sago-based products and to assist small scale enterprises, at village level.

Traditional sago preparation methods were investigated in Papua New Guinea and in neighbouring countries. After research and testing, 'Sago Pops' were introduced to women's groups in the Sepik River Basin. Sago Pops are a snack product made from sago slices which are first steamed, then dried and finally fried in hot oil to produce a ready-to-eat-food. This particular region was identified because sago was plentiful.

The women were initially reluctant to accept a sago product which was processed in a way they were unaccustomed to. After seeing that sago could be made into attractive products which could compete with imported foods, they became interested to learn these new processing techniques.

A year later it was found that Sago Pops had become well known in the region and that several village-level enterprises had developed. This case study is cited in order to highlight the possibilities of transferring traditional processing technologies from one country to another. However, before pursuing such an approach, it is vital that local consumption habits and taste preferences are thoroughly investigated. (New, 1986)

5
Planning a project or enterprise

FROM the selection of case studies presented in Chapter 4, some questions emerge which should be asked by project planners and decision makers before they proceed with the implementation of a processing project or promotion of a root crop processing enterprise.

Some questions, particularly socio-economic issues, are of fundamental importance and must be addressed in baseline data or feasibility studies at the initial stages of project planning. Looking at the questions below may draw attention to areas where more information is needed before project implementation can go ahead. Other questions, particularly those concerned purely with technical information, may be answered (having carried out the initial studies) with simple one- or two-sentence or yes/no answers.

The first questions are concerned with the viability of the enterprise; then there are questions about the role of women in traditional processing, with subsidiary questions listed below the main question where appropriate; and finally the impact of improved technologies is considered.

First questions

1. Why set up a small-scale root crop processing venture?
   o Is there a market for increased yields?
   o Can the existing system cope with increased demand?
   o If yes to the above, how will you improve/add capacity?
2. When processing a given quantity of roots or tubers using the traditional process, what inputs are required?
   o How much time is required?
   o What is the labour input required by male and female labour for each activity or stage?
   o How much fuel is used, and is it readily available?
   o How much is yielded?
   o What is the value of the inputs (raw materials, fuel, water, packaging) in comparison with the output?

Background questions

1. What exactly is the place of women in traditional processing? What role do they play in the different stages?
   o What is the traditional marketing mechanism and who controls it? (Do women have access to markets?)

o What proportion of the income from the processed root crop do women earn and keep?

o What are the major problems and difficulties of women producers in this field?

2. What is the extent of traditional and small-scale root crop processing in the area?

o What are the traditional processes?

o Which method tends to be used most frequently, and why?

o Does the main method vary in different parts of the country?

(It is important to know about the various traditional methods being used, as this may influence the improvements needed.)

3. Who owns the raw material?

o Are there more raw materials available than can be processed in the traditional manner?   Yes ☐   No ☐

o Are there ever seasonal shortages of raw materials?   Y ☐   N ☐

o What is done with the by-products, if any?

Effects of improved technology on traditional processing industry

Technical considerations

1. Will the use of the improved technology reduce labour input as compared with the traditional method? How?

2. What is the capacity of the improved technology — will it be able to cope with the demands of processing in terms of quantity of material available to processors?

3. Will the equipment produce a greater quantity and better quality end product than traditional means? (Will the end product have a different taste — if so, will it be acceptable?)

4. What will be the processing rate?

5. Will the process be faster?   Y ☐   N ☐

6. What are the water/fuel/power requirements of the equipment?

7. Will the users be able to meet those requirements?   Y ☐   N ☐

8. Will use of the equipment require a change in packaging Y ☐   N ☐ or transport of the material?   Y ☐   N ☐

9. If power-driven equipment is being introduced, can the users meet the electrical/diesel requirements on a regular basis?   Y ☐   N ☐

10. Are there alternative energy sources?   Y ☐   N ☐

11. Are there means of producing equipment and/or spares locally?   Y ☐   N ☐

12. Can the equipment be maintained using local resources?

o are spare parts available?   Y ☐   N ☐

o can local artisans repair the machinery Y ☐   N ☐ or do they need to be trained? Y ☐   N ☐

13. Will the users be able to afford the cost of the spare parts? Y ☐   N ☐

o will they need technical training Y ☐   N ☐ and if so, how much?

o is training locally available? Y ☐   N ☐

o is there already some familiarity with this type of technology? Y ☐   N ☐

Socio-economic considerations

1. What is the cost of the machine and related equipment?
2. Is the cost manageable on an individual or community basis?
3. If credit is needed is it accessible? Will the women be able to repay the loan?
4. What will the return on the investment be? What will the monthly profit be?
5. How many years will it take the operator to cover the cost of the machine?
6. Who will control use of the machine? Will it be co-operatively controlled or will individual men or women manage it?
7. Who will earn the income after processing?
8. Will availability of the improved technology increase women's income generation?
   - if not, why not?
   - what proportion of the income will women earn?
   - will root crop processing remain a significant income generating activity for women after introduction of the machine?
9. Will introduction of the equipment bring about any change in the pattern of work and work habits? How?
   - male
   - female
10. Will there be a change in the daily schedule required to do any task?
11. Does the improved equipment require more or less raw material than traditional methods?
12. If it requires more, is that supply available and who owns it?
13. Will the improved method change the traditional market mechanisms?
14. If more roots/tubers are processed, can the market cope with the increase and will this affect the price?
15. What will happen to any by-products from the improved method?
16. If by-products are sold, who will earn the income?
17. Will the users be able to cope with the consequential requirements of effective enterprise development such as handling employees, market and price negotiations, and cash flow?

References

Bo-Pujehun Agricultural Programme (1984) *Gari Industry in Bo-Township*. Report, Series No. 23.

Bo-Pujehun Rural Development Project (1986) *Profile of Women in Farming Systems*, Occasional Paper No. 4.

Bruinsma, Wirtsenburg and Wirdemann (1983) *Selection of technologies for food processing in developing countries*. Wageningen, Netherlands

Cooke, R.V. (1978) 'Cassava and the cyanide problem'. *West African Technical Review*, January, pp. 67–71.

FAO (1984) *FAO Year Book*.

Horton, D.E., Fano, H. (1985) *Potato atlas*. CIP, p. 52.

ILO (1987) *Gari processing. Technologies for rural women — Ghana*. Technical manual No. 4 ILO/Government of Netherlands/National Council of Women and Development, Ghana.

ILO/NCWD (1987) *Technologies for Rural Women — Ghana*, Technical Manual No. 4, ILO/National Council on Women and Development, Accra.

Momoh, M., Frey-Nakonz, R., Bauer, E. (1984) *Gari industry in Bo township. Bo-Pujehun rural development project, agricultural programme*. Report Series No. 23.

New, R. (1986) *The development of Sago products in Papua New Guinea*. Appropriate Technology Development Institute, Lae, Papua New Guinea.

Rivera-Ortiz, J. M., Gonzalez, M.A. (1972) 'Lye peeling of fresh yam, *dioscorea alata*'. *Journal of Agriculture of University of Puerto Rico*, Vol. 56, No. 1, pp. 57–63.

Williams, C.E. (1982) 'The effect of technological innovation among rural women in Nigeria; a case study of gari processing in selected villages of Bendel State, Nigeria.' *Journal of Rural Development*, No. 5.

Further reading

Adams, E. (1987) 'Taro varieties and their uses in the Pacific Island States'. *The Courier*, No. 101, pp. 92–93.

Adekanye in Ahmed, I. (ed.) (1985) *Innovation and rural women in Nigeria: cassava processing and food production*. Technology and Rural Women.

Akorada, M. (1987) 'Yam, sweet potato and cocoyam'. *The Courier*, No. 101, pp. 78–81.

ATI (1986) 'Potato based food products in Peru'. *Appropriate Technology International Bulletin*, No. 7.

Bennison, H. (1987) 'Cassava: its developing importance'. *The Courier*, No. 101, pp. 69–71.

Boccas, B. (1987) 'Cassava: staple food of prime importance in the tropics'. *The Courier*, No. 101, pp. 72–73.

Booth, R.H., Wholey, D.W., in Weber, E.J., Cock, J.H., Chouinard, A. (eds.) (1978) 'Cassava processing in southeast Asia'. In: *Cassava harvesting and processing*. Proceedings of a workshop held at CIAT, Cali, Colombia. IDRC, Ottawa, pp. 7–11.

Carruthers, I. and Rodriguez, M. (1992) *Tools for Agriculture: A guide to appropriate equipment for smallholder farmers*. IT Publications, London.

Cedillo, V.G. (1982) 'Cassava Rice or Landang'. *The Philippine Agriculturalist,* Vol. 35, No. 8, pp. 434–440.

CERES (1979) 'Another look at potato's potential in infant diets'. *Ceres,* Vol. 12, No. 6.

CERES (1980) 'A plea for the potato'. *Ceres,* Vol. 14, No. 1.

Chan, H.T., Jr. (ed.) (1983) *Handbook of tropical foods*. Marcel Dekker, Inc., New York.

Charbonneau, R. (1986) *Just add potatoes: enriching the Peruvian diet*. IDRC Reports, Vol. 15, No. 2.

Coursey, D.G. (1965) *The role of yams in West African food economics,* reprinted from *World Crops.* Grampian Press Ltd, London.

Coursey, D.G., Ferber, C.E.M., in Plucknett, D.L. (ed.) (1979) 'The processing of yams'. In *Small-scale processing and storage of tropical root crops*. Westview Press, Boulder, Colorado, pp. 189–211.

Coursey, D.G. (1982) 'Traditional tropical root crop technology: some interactions with modern science'. *IDS Sussex Bulletin,* Vol. 13, No. 3, pp. 12–20.

Coursey, D.G. in Chat, H.T. Jr. (ed.) (1983) 'Yams'. In *Handbook of Tropical Foods*. Marcel Dekker Inc., New York.

Coursey, D.G. in Terry, E.R., Doku, E.V., Arene, O.B., Mahjungu, N.M. (ed.) (1984) *Potential utilisation of major root crops with special emphasis on human, animal and industrial uses*. *Tropical Root Crops: Production and Uses in West Africa*. Proceedings of Second Triennial Symposium, International Society Tropical Crops. Doula, Cameroon, pp. 25–35.

Coursey, D.G. (Undated) 'Food technology and the yam in West Africa'. *Tropical Science,* Vol. VIII, No. 4.

Coursey, D.G., Booth, R.H. (Undated) *Contributions of postharvest technology to trade to tropical root crops*. Tropical Products Institute, London.

Crabtree, J., Kramer, E.C., Baldrey, J. (1978) 'The breadmaking potential of products of cassava as partial replacements for wheat flour'. *Journal of Food Technology,* Vol. 13, pp.397–407.

De Vries, C.A., Ferwado, J.D., Flach, M. (1967) 'Choice of food crops in relation to actual and potential production in the tropics'. *Netherlands Journal of Agricultural Science,* Vol. 15, pp. 241–248.

Dendy, D.A.V., James, A.W., Clarke, P.A. (1970) *Work of the Tropical Products Institute on the use of non-wheat flours in breadmaking*. Proceedings of a symposium on the use of non-wheat flour in bread and baked goods manufacture. G62, Tropical Products Institute, London.

Dupont, J. (1983) *Yams have their reasons*. IDRC Reports, Vol. 12, No. 2.

Durrant, N. (1987) 'The pre-eminence of roots and tubers in the diets of the Caribbean peoples'. *The Courier,* No. 101, pp. 89–91.

Etejere, E.O., Bhat, R.B. (1985) *Traditional preparation and uses of cassava in Nigeria*. *Economics Botany,* Vol. 39, No. 2, pp. 157–164.

Ezekwe, G.O. (undated) *Mechanizing the peeling of cassava and yam*. University of Nigeria, Nsukka.

FAO (1981) *Food loss prevention in perishable crops.* FAO Agricultural Services Bulletin, No. 43, Rome.

Fellows, P. and Hampton, A. (1992) *Small-scale Food Processing: A guide to appropriate equipment.* IT Publications, London.

Fresco, L.O. (1986) *Cassava in shifting cultivation: a systems approach to agricultural technology development in Africa.* Royal Tropical Institute, The Netherlands.

Fleury, J.M. (1980) *Message to agronomists: more than agronomic factors must be taken into account when promoting cassava in developing countries.* The IDRC Reports, Vol. 9, No. 2.

Fomunyam, R.P., Adegdola, A.A., Oke, O.L. (1980) *The role of palm oil in cassava-based rations. Tropical root crops research strategies for the 1980s.* Proceedings of first triennial root crops symposium. Ibadan, Nigeria, pp. 152–153.

Gebremeskel, T., Oyewole, D.B. (1987) *Cocoyam in Africa and the world trends of vital statistics 1965–1984.*
Socio-economic Unit, International Institute of Tropical Agriculture, Nigeria.

Grace, M.R. (1977) *Cassava Processing.* FAO Plant Production and Protection Series, No. 3, Rome.

Horton, D.E. (1987) 'Potatoes in the Third World'. *The Courier,* No. 101, pp.82–84.

Hoover, M.W., Miller, N.C. (1973) 'Process for producing sweet potato chips.' *Food Technology.*

Horton, D., Lynam, J., Knipscheer, H. (undated) *Root crops in developing countries — An economic appraisal.*

Ihekoronye, A.I., Ngoddy, P.O. (1985) *Integrated food science and technology for the tropics.* Macmillan Publishers Ltd, London, pp. 266–270.

IITA – UNICEF (1986) *Cassava — a crop for household security: a 1986 situation analysis for Oro local area — Nigeria.* Socio-economic Unit, International institute of Tropical Agriculture, Nigeria.

ILO (1984) *Improved village technology for women's activities: a manual for West Africa.* ILO/Government of Norway.

Ingram, J.S. (1977) *Cassava processing: commercially available machinery.* TPI Report. G75.

Kwatia, J.T. (1986) *Cassava: storage, processing, and utilization.* IITA/UNICEF consultation on the promotion of household food production and nutrition.

Kwatia, J.T. (1986) *Report on the existing cassava storage and processing techniques in Southern Nigeria with a view of making recommendations for the establishment of rural cassava processing and utilization centres.* UNICEF/IITA collaborative programme for household food security and nutrition.

Lancaster, P.A., Ingram, J.S.m, Lim, M.Y., Coursey, D.G. (1982) 'Traditional cassava-based foods: survey of processing techniques'. *Economic Botany,* Vol. 36, No. 1, pp. 12–45.

Lancaster, P.A., Coursey, D.G. (1978) 'Traditional post harvest technology of perishable tropical staples'. *FAO Agricultural Services Bulletin,* No. 59.

Larley, B.L. (1970) 'A prototype cassava grater for use in Ghana, based on studies of existing graters.'
Ghana Journal of Agricultural Science, Vol. 3, pp. 53–59.

Levi, S.S., Oruche, C.B. (1958) *Some inexpensive improvements in village scale gari making.* Research Report No. 2, Federal Ministry of Commerce and Industry, Lagos, Nigeria.

Loftas, T. (1987) 'Essential elements in nutrition'. *The Courier*, No. 101, pp. 66–68.

Lopez De V., A.M. (1985) 'Cassabe, the cassava bread'. *Cassava Newsletter*, Vol. 9, No. 2, pp. 1–3.

Martin, F.W. (1983) *Women's role in root and tuber crops production*. Expert consultation of women in food production 7–14 December. FAO ESH: WIFP/83/16.

May J.H., Nip, W.K. (1983) *Taro: A review of colocasia esculenta and its potential*, pp.261–268.

Obiakor, E.K., Chiori, C.O. (Undated) *Pretreatment of cassava tubers in hot 'lye' solution for mechanized peeling*. Faculty of Engineering, University of Benin, Benin City, Nigeria and Department of Pharmacy, University of Nigeria, Nsukka, Nigeria.

Odigboh, E.U., in Plucknett, D.L. (ed.) (1979) *Mechanical devices for peeling cassava roots*. In *Small-scale processing and storage of tropical root crops*. Westview Press, Boulder, Colorado, USA.

Rickard, J.E. (1983) 'Post harvest problems of tropical root crops'. *Alafua Agricultural Bulletin*, Vol. 8, No. 2, pp. 65–72.

Terry, E.R., Doku, E.V., Arene, D.B., Mahungu, N.M. (1984) *Tropical root crops: production and uses in Africa*, IDRC-221e.

Werge, R.W. (1978) 'Potato processing in the central highlands of Peru'. *Ecology of food and nutrition*. Vol. 7, pp. 229–234.

Williams, C.E., in Plucknett, D.L. (ed.) (1979) 'The role of women in cassava processing in Nigeria'. In *Small-scale processing and storage of tropical root crops*. Westview Press, Boulder, Colorado, USA, pp. 340–353.

Contacts

The following can be contacted for further information on root crop processing, equipment and experiences in planning root crop processing projects. Some of these institutions have developed their own equipment which has been or is being used in the field.

Agricultural Engineering Department
University of Nigeria, West Africa

Agricultural Engineering Department
University of Science and Technology, Kumasi, Ghana, West Africa

Agrico, Agricultural Engineers Ltd
Ring Road Industrial Area, PO Box 12127, Accra North, Ghana, West Africa

ATI
Appropriate Technology International, 1331 H Street N.W., Washington DC 20005, USA

CIAT
Centro Internacional de Agricultura Tropical, Apartado Aereo 67–13, Cali, Valle del Caura, Colombia

CIP
The International Potato Center,
Apartado 5969, Lima, Peru, South America *or*
c/o Tropical Africa Region, PO Box 25171, Nairobi, Kenya

Crypto Peerless Ltd
Bordesley Green Road, Birmingham B9 4UA, UK

CTCRI
Central Tuber Crops Research Institute, Sreekariyan, Trivandrum, 695015 Kerala, India

Department of Agricultural Chemistry and Food Science
University of Philippines, Diliman, Q.C. 3004, Philippines

Department of Agricultural Engineering
Njala University College, Freetown, Sierra Leone, West Africa

Department of Tropical Crop Science
PO Box 341, Wageningen 6700 AH, The Netherlands

FAO
United Nations Food and Agricultural Organization, Via delle Terme di Caracalla, 00100 Rome, Italy

FABRICO
The Fabrication and Production Company, Asaba, S.W. Nigeria

FIIR
The Federal Institute of Industrial Research, Oshodi, Lagos, S.W. Nigeria

GATE/GTZ
German Appropriate Technology Exchange, Postfach 5180, D-6236 Eschborn 1, Germany

IDRC
International Development Research Centre, PO Box 8500, Ottawa K1G 3H9, Canada

IITA
International Institute of Tropical Agriculture, PMB 5320, Ibadan, Nigeria

ITDG
Intermediate Technology Development Group, Myson House, Railway Terrace, Rugby CV21 3HT, UK

Nardi Francesco & Figli
06017 Seici Lama, Perugia, Italy

NRI
Natural Resources Institute, Central Avenue, Chatham Maritime, Chatham ME4 4TB, UK

Philippine Root Crop Research and Training Centre
Visayas State College of Agriculture, Bay Bay, Leyte 7127 Philippines

PRODA
The Production Development Agency, 3 Independence Layout, PO Box 609, Enugu, Anambra State, Nigeria

P. T. Kerta Laksana
J1 Jenderal Sudirman 504, Bandung, Indonesia

Root Crop Research Institute
Umudike, Umuahia, Imo State, Nigeria

Royal Tropical Institute (KIT)
Mauritskade 63, 1092 AD Amsterdam, Netherlands
Rural Agro-Industrial Development Scheme
11 University Crescent, PMB 5517, Ibadan, Oyo State, Nigeria, West Africa
TAEC
Tikonko Agricultural Extension Centre, c/o Methodist Church Headquarters, Wesley
House, PO Box 64, Freetown, Sierra Leone, West Africa
TCC
Technology Consultancy Centre, University of Science and Technology Kumasi, Ghana,
West Africa

A range of hand- and machine-operated mills suitable for different scales of operation
are available from:

Ndume Products Ltd
PO Box 6, Gilgil, Kenya, East Africa